CASTLES

An Enduring Fantasy

CA

Edited by
Naomi Reed Kline

STLES

An Enduring Fantasy

Aristide D. Caratzas,
Publisher
1985

Published by:
Aristide D. Caratzas, Publisher
Caratzas Publishing Co., Inc.
P.O. Box 210 (481 Main Street)
New Rochelle, N.Y. 10802

International Standard Book Number:
0-89241-374-3

Library of Congress Catalog Card Number:
83-21040

**Library of Congress Cataloging in Publication
Data**
Main entry under title: Castles: An Enduring Fantasy
1. Castles in art - Addresses, essays, lectures. 2. Castles
in literature - Addresses, essays, lectures.
3. Arts - Addresses, essays, lectures. I. Kline,
Naomi Reed.
BX650.C29C37   1985   700   83-21040

*The publication of this book was made possible, in part, by
a grant from the National Endowment for the
Humanities, Washington, D.C.*

Preface Americans have long been fascinated by the Middle Ages and by the castle, symbol and archetype of the medieval period. Despite the geographic separation of the New World from medieval Europe, castles punctuate the American landscape and have penetrated the American state of mind as a focus for fantasy and romance. But the 'mythologizing' of castles is neither a new nor a strictly American development. The castle has been a foil for the imagination since the first castles were built. The attributes of monumental strength and grandeur, which stemmed from the castle's first function as a military stronghold and later grew as castles became economic and political centers, conferred real power and prestige on castle-owners. Medieval art and allegory further amplified the castle's symbolic aspect to 'mythic' proportions, and the castle became the site of the idylls of the age of courtly love.

Because of these powerful associations, castles have never ceased to be built nor have they lost their symbolic allure. In more recent times, castles have figured largely in tales for children and adults, in paintings and drawings, and thus have contributed further material for our dreams and fantasies. From medieval romances to contemporary illustrated children's books — from the Tower of London to the castles of Disney's playgrounds — castles have captured the popular imagination.

This volume, an exploration of the romance of castles, is intended as an introduction to the endlessly intriguing realm of castle imagery. It concentrates primarily on castles as they appear in art, literature, and architecture, within historical contexts. It is divided into three parts, each covering a broad chronological period: the Middle Ages (circa 1100 through 1500) in *The Age of Chivalry*; the eighteenth and nineteenth centuries in *The Gothic Revival*; and the mid-nineteenth century to our own day in *The Popular Explosion*. In each section, knowledgeable authors discuss aspects of our fascination with castles and, by extension, with the Middle Ages in general. Each section is provided with an introduction that sets the tone for the essays to follow. In essays dealing with later responses to the Middle Ages, the focus is mainly on England and

America — where the Gothic Revival began and later flourished.

It is appropriate that this book has grown out of a project of the Hammond Castle Museum in Gloucester, Massachusetts. Built in the 1920s by the inventor John Jay Hammond, Jr., this American castle was the site, in 1982, of an exhibition entitled "Castles: An Enduring Fantasy." The exhibition explored some of the ways in which castles have, through art, literature, and architecture, affected our thinking. Although many of the works of art illustrated here appeared in the exhibition, the essays have been written especially for this book.

Research for and publication of this book were made possible by two grants from the National Endowment for the Humanities. In 1980, with the support of the first grant, a team of scholars in various disciplines within the humanities was selected to help formulate the basic outlines of this book. Drs. Jill H. Adels, Patricia Dooley, Laila Z. Gross, Robin Miller, James F. O'Gorman, and James Welu were members of the original group and were especially generous with their time and ideas.

The second grant, awarded in 1981, made it possible to expand the planned volume to incorporate additional scholarly essays and to engage expert editorial help in organizing the manuscript. I would like to thank Barbara Gale, George Rosen, and Marybeth Sollins for their invaluable editorial services. The book in its final form reflects the varied efforts of all those involved in its planning and realization, and it crystallizes the goals of the "Castles" project.

Naomi Reed Kline

Contents

List of Illustrations

Naomi Reed Kline *The Age of Chivalry*

The castle — a strategically isolated stone building, bristling with turrets and crenellations, protected by moat and drawbridge — is an architectural dinosaur, the creature of a past era. But as an emblem of romance, it endures. A long literary tradition, beginning during the medieval period itself, has contributed to the illusion that within the castle's charmed confines a world of chivalry and honor prevailed. Literature has, in fact, often overshadowed the reality of these startling monuments.

The images of the world of Camelot and knightly chivalry which appeal so strongly to the imagination have often eclipsed what is perhaps the most important aspect represented by the medieval castle — the aspect of feudal authority. If we are to understand the power of castles in the world of the imagination, we must turn first to the reality of the castle during the Middle Ages — to the facts on which the later fictions were built.

Life in medieval times was closely tied to two architectural centers, cathedral and castle. Whereas cathedrals were built to ensure eternal rewards transcending the brutality of life, castles provided feudal society with the more tangible requirement of temporal refuge. Feudalism was based on fealties (obligations of loyalty) and responsibilities that bound members of society to an immediate overlord. A communal effort was generally required to support a military stronghold capable of providing security for the community. In exchange for the lord's protection, individuals were obliged to fulfill military duties for specified periods and, in varying degrees, to contribute money and goods to the lord's coffers.

Throughout continental Europe in the centuries that followed the fall of Rome in 410, the complexity of allegiances that bound subordinates to overlords transformed the Roman *castrum*, which represented an ideal of city planning, into the medieval *castel* or village. But by the year 1100, the word *castel*, in both French and Middle English, specifically referred to a fortress stronghold. This shift of meaning took place in the wake of the dramatic defeat of the English by William, Duke of Normandy (William the Conqueror), at Hastings in 1066. The Conquest led to an unprecedented proliferation of castles swiftly erected to provide military and administrative bases for the development of Norman feudalism on Anglo-Saxon soil.

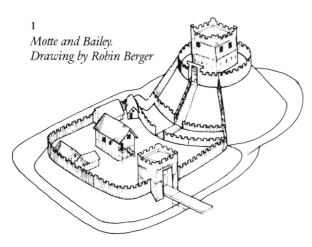

1
Motte and Bailey.
Drawing by Robin Berger

2
Opposite page:
Tower of London.
Photograph: Paola Piglia

3
Rochester Castle, Kent.
Photograph courtesy of
the British Tourist Authority.

What did these early castles look like? Typically they were crude earthwork fortresses of the type called motte and bailey (fig. 1). The first line of defense was the bailey, a large courtyard surrounded by a ditch. Usually a bridge connected this area to the motte, an embankment palisaded around the summit and base and surmounted by a wooden tower. The motte was the castle's second and ultimate line of defense. In their reliance upon timber instead of stone, these castles had a more primitive appearance than the more monumental castles that, to a large extent, were soon to replace them.

Although William the Conqueror solidified his control of England with timbered mottes and baileys, stone masonry replaced the wooden palisades by the end of the eleventh century. The famous Tower of London (fig. 2) and the stone keep at Rochester (fig. 3), for instance, bear testimony to the permanence of continued Norman ambitions.

Norman castles, architectural symbols of the feudal order, tied England to a continental Europe that was already dotted with crenellated walls. By the twelfth century, the European game of power was being played out through the seizure and control of castle fortresses. In France, the monarchy was consolidating its power through constant political and military maneuvers. King Frederick I, Barbarossa, of the Holy Roman Empire, reasserted his imperial rights in Italy, made Swabia the center of the enlarged empire, and punctuated this extended territory with approximately three hundred and fifty palaces and castles. In this manner he was the inheritor of the family tradition of castle building, for it was said of his grandfather, Frederick of Swabia that "[he] always drags a fortress with him at the tail of his horse."[1] Beyond nationalistic boundaries, where the

4
*Crac des chevaliers
Syria, 12th-13th
century. Photograph
by Peter Fergusson.
Courtesy of Wellesley
College Art Department*

5
*Harlech Castle.
Photograph courtesy
of the British
Tourist Authority*

chessboard of Europe proved too confining, the Christian reconquest of Spain, and the Crusades, under the combined auspices of Church and State, gave the European powers opportunities for further expansion under the banner of liberating land from the infidels.

The crusaders returned to their homelands with memories of stone fortresses seen in Spain and the Levant (fig. 4). The strides made in the art of warfare as a result of what they had learned in the East — with a corresponding intensification of human suffering — triggered an expansion in the architectural vocabulary of the castle buildlers. Crenellations, machicolations, arrow loops, and barbicans became currency; the era of the fortified castle began in earnest.

By the latter part of the thirteenth century, England's Edward I had virtually subjugated the Welsh by building along the border a string of castles that were for all practical purposes impregnable. The very presence of his castles at Conway, Harlech (fig. 5), and Beaumaris, all constructed under the direction of James of St. George, Master of the King's Works, largely extinguished the sparks of insurrection in Wales.

With the reign of Edward I, the strategic value of the castle and military power of the lord it represented had become so overwhelming that the castle could perform its function simply by the fact of its existence. In this respect, the castles of Edward I are the quintessence of the functional medieval fortress. And it is at this point that it might be well to leave castle architecture and investigate the growing body of fiction that surrounded the castle itself.

The castle was the bastion of secular culture, the cradle and focus of medieval secular literature. It was within the castle walls that the idealization of noble life emerged. A code of chivalry was created first in literature, particularly under such enlightened patrons of the twelfth and thirteenth centuries as Eleanor of Aquitaine and her daughter, Marie, Countess of Champagne, and became in turn a force in social and cultural life. Much of this literature of the 'courtly' genre was created within the halls of castles where it was performed for the nobility. Tales of love and war, reaffirming communal values, resounded through the ceremonial spaces. To emphasize the supposed veracity of these works, the troubadors frequently included references to local landmarks and personages in their compositions.

Thus art became the vehicle for the romanticization of the castle, even during the medieval period itself. The chansons de geste, *of which fewer than one hundred survive from the*

6
Old Testament Miniature,
ca. 1250:
Saul Destroys Nahash
and the Ammonites.
Courtesy of the
Pierpont Morgan Library.
M. 638, f. 23v

eleventh through the fourteenth centuries, provide our primary evidence for this phenomenon. The chansons, *narrative poems which had grown out of centuries of oral composition chronicling legendary deeds of warfare and heroism, were broadly based on historical subjects (fig. 6). Troubadors and trouvères, the poets and singers of the period, and roving storytellers transformed Celtic, Frankish, and Teutonic myths into stories of feudal devotion and allegiance to the chivalric code. Through literature of this kind, tales of the Court of King Arthur and the history of Britain, as well as information about the world of Classical antiquity and the conflicts between Christendom and Islam, became accessible — first to noble audiences and later, with the rise of popular vernacular literature, to increasingly wider audiences.*

That this growing vernacular literature often spoke not of contemporary events, but of a more distant past, is important; for although innovations in structural engineering sometimes came close to providing ideal castle fortifications, life itself in the Middle Ages was far from ideal. Literary works represented, to some degree, the idealized fantasies of courtly poets who created the tradition of chivalry, transforming the barbarism of the actual past into a golden age peopled with the paladins of Charlemagne and the knights of the Round Table. The castle became the source of the romantic fantasies of its own age.

The theme of good versus evil dominated medieval imagery. The siege, a military reality, became a metaphor: the forces of evil were pitted against those of good, which were protected by the supposedly impregnable architectural symbol of the castle. In the Castle of Perseverance, *a fifteenth-century morality play, it is in the castle that man withstands his three enemies, the world, the flesh, and the Devil. The castle is described as a "precyous place, fful of vertu and of grace." [2] This concept had even earlier variations. For example, in the thirteenth-century religious poem,* Le songe de castel (The Dream of the Castle), *the forces of evil attack the castle under the leadership of the Seven Deadly Sins. In the end, death overcomes the castle, which is depicted as a representation of man.*

In the Roman de la rose (Romance of the Rose), *one of the most popular French secular poems of the Middle Ages, a castle is the fortress in which the rose, the symbol of love, is guarded; the castle is also the object of a siege by the God of Love and his vassals. This poem is just one of many works, though it was the first, to link symbolically the themes of love and war. Clearly one of the most powerful of chivalric literary conventions is the symbolic portrayal of the "Castle of Love" as the site of idealized love. This image recurs in the poetry and visual arts of the Middle Ages — even as late as the sixteenth century. The castle was seen as the home of the God of Love and as a place for lovers, protected from the toils of the outside world. Some of the many representations of the Castle of Love and its relation to the social functions of the real-life castle are explored by Laila Z. Gross in her essay,* The Castle of Love in Medieval Literature and Art.

Perhaps the most fitting of castle images was that of the enchanted castle, which partook of the symbolic aspects of impregnability and remoteness to an exaggerated degree. Magically visible from afar because of the splendor of its building materials, the enchanted castle was generally isolated from the world, situated in a forest, at the edge of water, perched on a rock, or even concealed underground. The tower, often without stairs or a door, figured prominently as the stronghold that separated the fairy world or world of fantasy from that of the real. Appropriately, the bridge and moat that linked these two worlds were the focus of tension in many of the stories in which this image was used.[3]

7

*Bracteate: Conrad III
of Hohenstaufen.
Courtesy of the American
Numismatic Society*

These are only a few of the rich variety of castle images and symbols to be found in medieval literature. Ironically, the proliferation of literary conceits in which the castle was the central image paralleled the growing military obsolescence of fortified castles. At least by the later twelfth century in northwestern Europe, the mechanical artillery of siege had reduced the role and value of the castle, in most cases, to that of personal protection and a symbol of prestige. Interestingly one finds, from existing licenses to crenellate, that as early as the twelfth century the right to battlement or crenellate a building was rather more likely to be bestowed as a recognition of an overlord's favor than as a military prerogative.[4]

Few castles, crenellated or not, were ever truly siege-worthy. Although most were capable of deterring the enemy for brief periods, only a select few (e.g., those of Edward I), were capable of resisting the prolonged offensive measures of a well-equipped and organized attack. And indeed by the fourteenth century, even sieges were superseded in large part by open warfare, so that castles were, to a large degree, divorced from military function.

The asceticism of military demands gave way to the more sumptuous requirements of comfort. Where arrow loops alone once pierced the walls, there were now broad windows with wider vistas. By the late fourteenth and early fifteenth centuries, the function of the castle had become more civil than military. But the strength of the symbol remained. In the world of literature and myth the romantic associations of chivalry continued to be attached to buildings that became primarily administrative centers and ostentatious symbols of power and wealth. Castles continued to be built with moats and drawbridges, crenellations and multiple towers. These elements, often exaggerated, harked back to a time when they had a purpose, when form and function seemed perfectly attuned to military requirements.

Symbols of such intrinsic power are difficult to eradicate from the human consciousness. Castles continued to be built, as emblems of wealth, power, and continuity, and castles of abstract design were stamped on coins (fig. 7) and seals as icons of authority. As James A. Welu explains in his essay, Castles on Maps, *the castle remained the universally understood cartographical symbol for the town for centuries after castles themselves were no longer fortified centers of population. Isolated elements of castle architecture — fortified city gates or crenellated curtain walls — came to represent the entire symbolic complex of the castle. With the growth and diversity of an expanding*

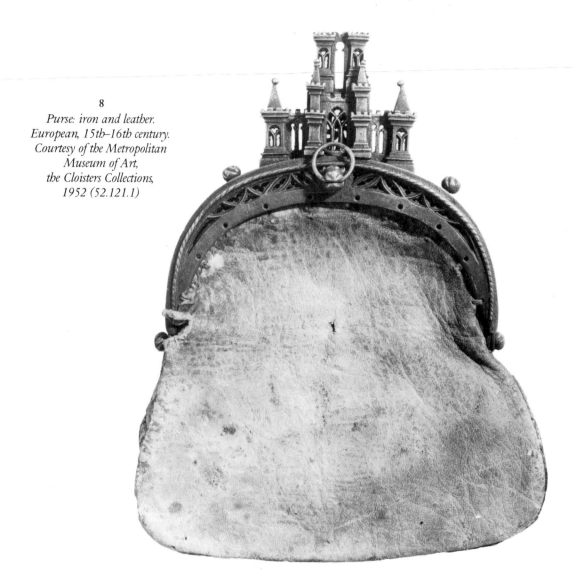

8
Purse: iron and leather.
European, 15th–16th century.
Courtesy of the Metropolitan
Museum of Art,
the Cloisters Collections,
1952 (52.121.1)

economy, an item as modest as the clasp of a lady's purse could serve as an ornamental reminder of the power of the castle (fig. 8).

Perhaps the search for permanence in a changing world provides the rationale for the endurance of the castle-image, so clearly documented in the following essays. This is displayed, perhaps most strikingly, in the fifteenth-century manuscript illuminations of the Très riches heures of the Duke de Berry, in which life unfolds before a backdrop of turreted castles (fig. 9). The diversions of the aristocracy and the responsibilities of the peasants follow the calendar's cycle while, in the background, the monumental castle represents a constant proof of wealth and authority — a dream of permanence in an impermanent and changing world.

10

9 10
Septembre. Août.
From the Très riches *From the* Très riches
heures du Duc de Berry. heures du Duc de Berry.
Courtesy of Musée Condé, *Courtesy of Musée Condé,*
Chantilly *Chantilly*

*The Castle of Love
in Medieval
Literature and Art*

Laila Z. Gross

J ust as the castle dominated the landscape and most people's lives in the Middle Ages, so it dominated thought and art (fig. 10). The period's felicitous ability to see things not just as themselves, but also as symbols for other things or ideas, meant that the image of the castle provided countless associations and interpretations. The strong exterior of the medieval castle evoked associations of power and impregnability. The interior of the castle promised elegance, ease, and love to the artistic imagination. Indeed, of all symbolic images that the real medieval castles inspired, few were as charming and as fully developed as the Castle of Love.

While the image of the Castle of Love is based on the actual medieval castle, what it came to stand for is the ultimate dream of love. Most love poems from the Middle Ages are set in the framework of a dream vision. From the first and most influential love narrative, *The Romance of the Rose* by the thirteenth-century French poet Guillaume de Lorris, to the fourteenth-century *Parliament of Fowls* by Geoffrey Chaucer, the poet and would-be lover falls asleep and dreams of love. And while each dreamer's vision of love differs slightly, literary and artistic conventions of the period provided writers and artists with many specific details of the visions of love.

The Castle of Love, as described in medieval literature and depicted in medieval art, has certain special characteristics. It is situated in a beautiful, flowering meadow or a garden that is usually compared to Paradise. The season is always spring or early summer, as the innumerable flowers and birds singing songs of love suggest. The walls of the castle are strong and thick, made — like everything else in the castle — of fabulous and dazzling materials such as ruby, porphyry, or ivory. The gates are usually made of solid gold, and the pillars may be blue enamel.

In keeping with the age's symbolic turn of mind, a poet describing the Castle of Love may move easily from a wall made of ruby to the drawbridge made of "sweet Breton lais [songs]" and a moat of "lovers' sighs of complaint." Strict logic has no place in such fantasies. Just as the poet

11
*Tapestry: Two Lovers.
French, 16th century.
Courtesy of the
Metropolitan Museum of Art,
Bequest of Mary Stillman
Harkness, 1950*

did not usually describe the whole castle, but used a few well-chosen details to evoke the whole, so in the visual representations a similar kind of shorthand is often used: a castle gate, a tower, a wall, or even a throne is enough to suggest the whole Castle of Love.

The inside of the castle is even more spectacular than the outside. The stained-glass windows show pairs of famous lovers, such as Tristan and Iseult, Lancelot and Guenevere, Paris and Helen. The tapestries on the walls, or wall paintings, also portray pairs of lovers in brilliant colors (fig. 11). The benches and beds are covered with fabulous silks from the Orient, woven in patterns that show the lives of famous lovers. Usually the floors of the Castle of Love are strewn with flowers, but in one poem a mosaic of precious stone "paints" flowers and wild beasts. Thus the garden or the glade, a conventional setting for romance, is brought indoors.

The gatekeeper, usually called Idleness, holds the key to the gate of the Castle of Love. Her name is appropriate, since one cannot play at the game of love — the only occupation allowed in the castle — if one is beset by cares or, worse, has to work. Those admitted through the gate of the Castle of Love are all in their youth, and they move "two by two." Old Age is specifically excluded, as are Envy, Anger, Hypocrisy, and other unpleasant characters. Also kept out are the "villains" — those who do not understand or appreciate the game of love played in the castle. They are kept out at all costs, since the perverse natures of these jealous and sullen creatures always lead them to spoil the fun of others.

The owner of the castle is the God of Love, who is a beautiful winged man in the prime of his life. His crown, denoting his royal status, is often made of flowers, as is his clothing. Birds flutter around him, thereby reinforcing both the angelic and the vernal images. The God of Love most often sits on an ivory throne encrusted with gems, though he sometimes (especially in fourteenth-century art) sits in a tree. While a tree seems incongruous inside a castle, the tree-throne is appropriate in terms of the symbolic castle's own logic since it suggests the garden setting of romance, as well as an image of Paradise.

The God of Love's powerful weapon is his ivory bow. His arrow hits the eye and descends in a mysterious manner into the heart, where it remains forever. The wound is permanent, and no medicine, except the

12
Ivory Mirror Back:
Lady and Gentleman Playing Chess.
French, ca. 1320–1340.
Courtesy of the Cleveland
Museum of Art,
Purchase from the
J.H. Wade Fund

continued sight and presence of one's beloved, can help to assuage the pain. The God is a regal figure who personifies the power of love. His magnificent appearance and attire inspire fear, love, and loyalty. In deliberate associations with religion and feudalism, he is called "Our Lord." The lover becomes his liegeman and swears eternal loyalty to Love. As the perfect lover, he offers his heart willingly and joyfully to receive the wound.

Amid dazzling colors and depictions of lovers, the company at the Castle of Love is seen or described as playing at the Game of Love. They talk, they sing, they dance, or they play special word games such as "debates of love," "demands of love," and "the king who does not lie." Other playful activities involve physical contact — simple games with names such as "frog in the middle," "hot cockles," and "post and pillar."

Of all the games played in real and imaginary castles, chess is the one most often mentioned in literary accounts. At no time was the game of chess more popular than in the Middle Ages, when it was considered mainly a game of chance. (In one version a throw of the dice determined the move.) Poets often describe lovers playing at chess, dice, and backgammon, and many works of art depict two lovers engaged in a chess game (fig. 12).

While chess was the most popular game in reality and fantasy, in pure fantasy the most elaborate game, and the strangest game of them all, was the Siege of the Castle of Love. The poetic juxtaposition of arms and love has been a commonplace at least since Ovid wrote that "every lover is a soldier, and Cupid has his own camp."[1] But the way love and arms were combined in the Siege of the Castle of Love was new, and typical of medieval symbolism.

In this delightful fantasy the battle is between the sexes: the knights attack the Castle of Love, while the ladies defend it from above. The God of Love himself appears on the ramparts. Other knights scale the walls, helped and welcomed by the ladies. Some couples on top or in private corners have already found each other and have no further interest in the battle (fig.13).

That it is no ordinary siege can be seen from the ammunition used: roses. The rose has traditionally been considered the flower of love, but in the Middle Ages that flower was paramount as the symbol of love. Poets and artists never forgot that by rearranging the letters in *rose* one could form the word *eros.* Therefore, roses appear

frequently in the love games in art and poetry. Lovers present roses to their ladies who return them in the form of garlands. By crowning their lovers with these garlands the ladies indicate their acceptance of the offered love. The God of Love, too, often prefers a garland of roses to his bejeweled gold crown.

But nowhere are roses used in such profusion as in the scenes of the Siege of the Castle of Love. Ladies toss single roses and empty baskets of them on the attacking knights. The knights, in turn, summon all their formidable war machinery to throw roses up with catapults and to shoot them from crossbows. Even the shields and the helmets are decorated with roses, as are the horses' coverings.

14
The Castle of Love. *From* De nobilitatibus,
sapientiis et prudentiis regum,
*by Walter de Milemete. Bodleian Library,
Ms. Ch. 92, fol. 3v.
Courtesy of the Governing Body
of Christ Church, Oxford*

Just how strongly the Siege of the Castle of Love
captured the imagination can be seen from the numerous
visual renderings of it. Many of these scenes survive carved
in ivory, either on casket lids or on round mirror cases.
The Siege is also found in colorful illuminations in
manuscripts (fig. 14) and on tapestries and it appears in
brilliant enamel and gold on vessels which were placed on
cupboards and used at the table in castles. Unfortunately,
many of these objects have disappeared, but we know of
their existence from the detailed wills and inventories of
the aristocracy.

From tantalizingly brief contemporary allusions and a

few later descriptions we know that the Siege of the Castle of Love was also popular in the most ephemeral of all art forms, the pageant. Pageants were usually staged at important events, such as the king's entry into a city or a marriage celebration. One was held in Treviso, Italy, in 1214, where the ladies defended a specially constructed castle that was fortified on all sides with sable and ermine, scarlet brocade, and rich silks.

As late as the sixteenth century, the attacking knights at such a siege sang: *"Château d'amour, te veux-tu pas rendre?/ Veux-tu rendre, ou tenir bon?"* (Castle of Love will you surrender?/ Will you surrender or keep holding out?).[2] The poetry of the fourteenth century is filled with descriptions of the Sieges of the Castles of Love. The image was so familiar that it became a common metaphor for winning love, as can be seen from John Gower's casual lines in the *Confessio Amantis:* *"Bot as men sein, wher the herte is failed,/ Ther schal no castell ben assailed"* (But as men say, where the heart has given up/No castle needs to be attacked").[3]

In a related image combining themes of love and war, knights prove their worth to the ladies in a joust, with the Castle of Love in the background (fig. 15). The ladies watch from the ramparts or balconies above; pairs of lovers on the sides have eyes only for each other. Many romances make it clear that the joust is for love and for the ladies, and we are often told that the ladies fell in love while watching such displays of valor. The object and result of the joust is the same as for the Siege. As one fourteenth-century poet, Jacques Bretel, breathlessly writes of a joust in *Le Tournoi de Chauvency: "Tout escriant: 'Amours! Amours!'"* (All cried: "Love! Love!").

The dreams, associations, and longings of love were expressed by medieval poets and artists in terms of the powerful and suggestive image of the Castle of Love. The functional structure in a martial society was transformed — in art and literature — into a palace of pleasure. While the Castles of Love in poetry and art existed only in fantasy, by the fourteenth century they had begun to influence the design of real castles and the life led inside them. By the fifteenth century, nobles seriously engaged in the kinds of tournaments and jousts depicted in poetry and art and began to build castles based on artistic and literary images. And by the sixteenth century the original castle, a military outpost, had given way to the castle of pleasure.

15
Ivory Casket Lid:
A. Joust. French, 14th century.
Courtesy of the Walters
Art Gallery, Baltimore

James A. Welu *Castles on Maps*

Castles began appearing regularly on maps as far back as the late Middle Ages. These depictions of castles range from detailed renderings of specific buildings to what is perhaps their most common use: as a symbol for the town. The mapmaker's changing image of the castle reflects not only the overall development of cartographic ornamentation, but also how society viewed the castle during and after the Middle Ages.

Some of the earliest depictions are attributed to the English chronicler Matthew Paris of St. Albans Abbey. His maps of Britain, made around 1250 to illustrate his *History of England*, contain numerous battlemented structures representing castles, abbeys, and fortified towns. Well-known sites include London, Windsor (Windles/ho/res), Canterbury (Cantaur), and Dover (Dou'a) (fig. 16). Looking much like the drawings of a child, these castles, which consist of turrets and crenellated walls, are among the earliest conventional symbols in the history of mapmaking[1]. Their rigid, block-like forms suggest the imperviousness of the Norman stronghold, one of the hallmarks of thirteenth-century England. All the fortifications on Paris's map are shown in elevation, or from the side, while the rest of the map is drawn as if seen from overhead.

As maps became more detailed, their depictions of castles became more varied. The change is clear in the so-called Gough Map of Great Britain, an anonymous manuscript map made around 1350, a century after those of Paris. The Gough Map, drawn with east at the top, was the most accurate description of the British Isles at the time. A detail from this map (fig. 17) shows several castellated towns, the most prominent of which is London. This toy-like drawing, which by its relatively large scale indicates the town's importance, consists of a tower, a gate, a wall, and, behind these, a church. Though the design is quite simple, it includes such architectural details as the stonework in the walls and the differentiation between the round windows of the church and the narrow, vertical openings of the outside walls. The roofs are painted green, as is the area around the castle — which suggests a moat.

Another much simpler castle motif helps to define the

16

Top. Detail:
Map of Great Britain.
Matthew Paris, ca. 1250.
Photograph courtesy of
the British Library

17

Right. Detail:
Gough Map, ca. 1350.
Photograph courtesy
of the Bodleian Library,
Oxford

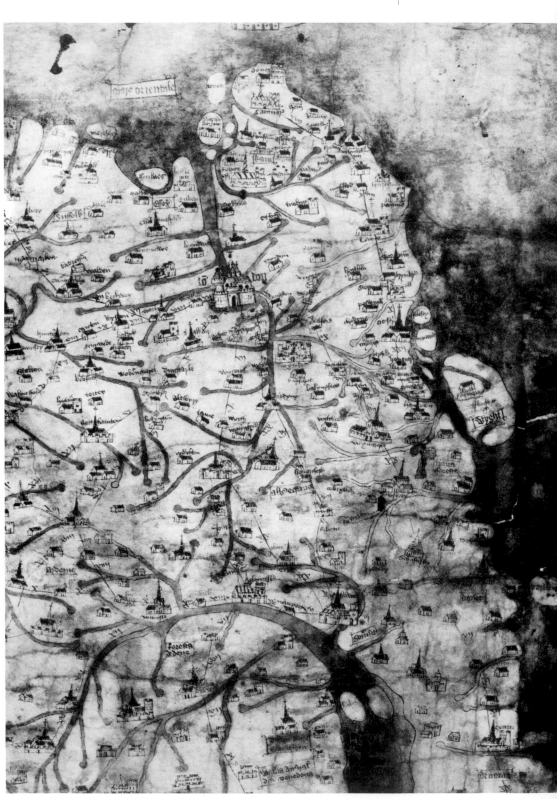

18

Detail:
Ebstorf Map, ca. 1284.
Courtesy of the Geography
and Map Division,
Library of Congress

status of some of the towns around London like Herford and Wallingford (walynford). Both are represented by a house and a tower, which refers to the twelfth-century castle in each of these towns. The castle at Windsor (wyndor) to the west of London — that is, below it on the map — includes much more detail. The mapmaker's drawing of the royal residence shows both the exterior wall with its gate and the internal structure with its crenellated towers.

Perhaps the most fanciful castle imagery appears on the ecclesiastical, or *T-O*, maps of the late Middle Ages. The name *T-O* refers to the fact that the three continents that make up these maps — Europe, Asia, and Africa — are arranged inside a circle in a pattern that resembles a *T*. Based primarily on Christian theology, these maps are drawn with east, or Asia, at the top. One of the largest and richest *T-O* maps is the famous Ebstorf map (circa 1284). Destroyed in World War II, it is named for the German monastery where it was discovered in 1832. A detail (fig. 18) shows several castle-like constructions in the area of Mesopotamia.

19
Sea Chart of the Mediterranean.
Vesconte Maggiolo, 1513.
Courtesy of the
Houghton Library,
Harvard University

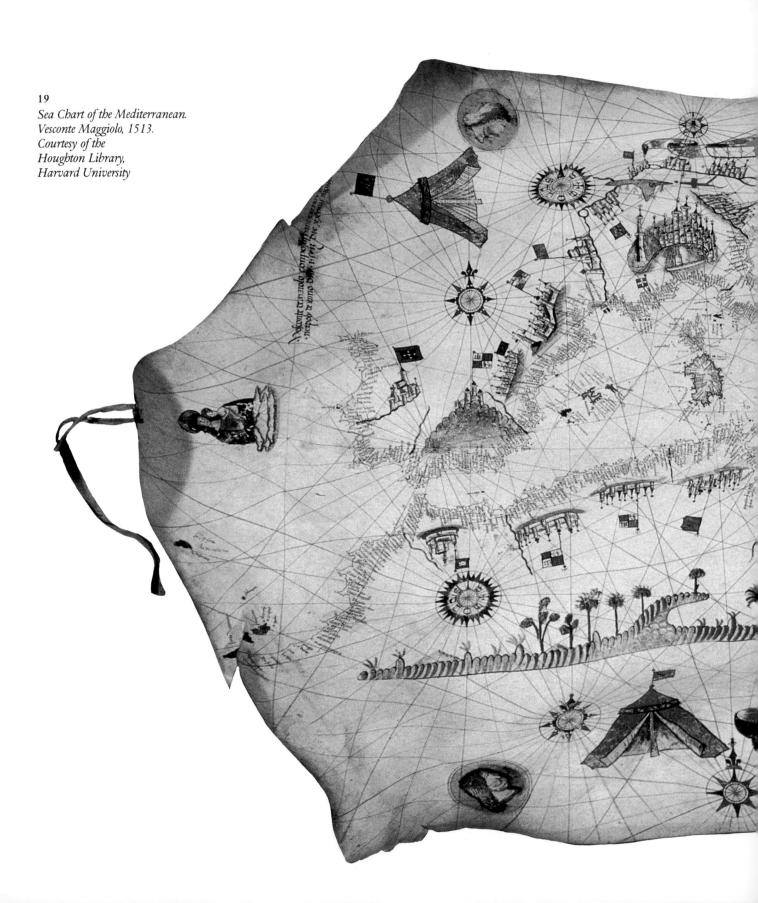

20
Illustration from
Traicté de l'usage
du Trigonometre.
Philippe Danfrie, 1597.
The John M.
Wing Collection.
Courtesy of
The Newberry Library,
Chicago

Though undoubtedly derived from architecture of the period, these buildings, like the map itself, are stylized; the majority represent fortified towns. As is typical in medieval art, the buildings are drawn as if seen from several angles. Equally abstract are the architectural details, which are reduced to decorative patterns and embellished with a wide range of colors (including gold leaf). Not surprisingly, one of the most prominent buildings on this essentially religious map represents Babylon. This ancient, biblical city, the largest on the Ebstorf map, lies on the Euphrates River, which on the map is appropriately shown flowing in one side of the castle-like structure and out the other. An inscription just above the city documents its legendary grandeur:

The great city of Babylon, the width of whose walls is 50 cubits [about 75 feet], height 200 cubits [about 300 feet]; its circumference 480 stadia [about 60 miles], fortified by 100 gates and with the Euphrates river flowing through its center. The great Nimrod laid the foundation for it, but Semiramis, queen of the Assyrians, embellished it and faced the wall with concrete and baked bricks.

At the same time that ecclesiastical maps were being produced, another, more accurate type of cartography — based on experiment and direct observation — began to appear; this was the portolan chart. These charts, which were made mainly in Catalonia and Italy, derive their name from the Italian word for sailing directions: *portolano*. Based on the use of the compass, they were designed to guide navigators as they traveled along the coasts. The earliest portolans date from around 1300, but this type of map continued to be made for centuries, with the most ornate examples appearing during the sixteenth century. It is these charts that contain the greatest number of depictions of castles and fortified towns.

In Vesconte Maggiolo's colorful chart of the Mediterranean, dated 1513 (fig. 19), the towns are represented by castles with numerous towers, which remind one of the imaginary structures found in books of fairy tales. None of the towns on Maggiolo's map can be identified by their architecture alone. Even Genoa, the mapmaker's hometown (shown in the area of northern Italy and southern Switzerland), is distinguished only by its famous harbor. Instead, each town flies a large banner bearing its coat of arms. At this period many towns were effectively individual nations, each controlling a small area of surrounding territory and often at rivalry with each other. This spirit of local autonomy is clearly demonstrated in Maggiolo's chart,

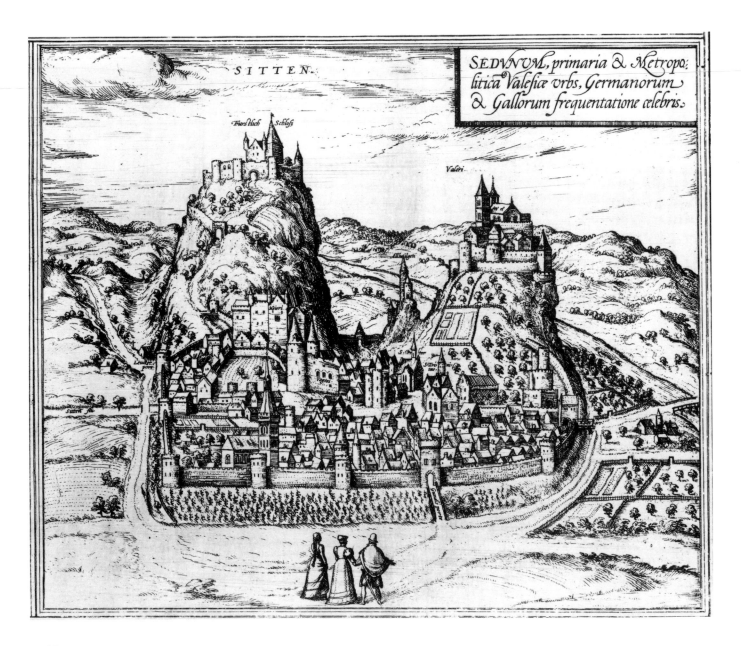

SITTEN.

SEDVNVM, primaria & Metropo:
litica Valesiæ vrbs, Germanorum
& Gallorum frequentatione celebris.

21
View of Sitten,
from Braun and Hogenberg
Civitates orbis
terrarum, *I, 1572. Courtesy of the*
Geography and Map Division,
Library of Congress

where each of the towns appears as a kingdom unto itself.

Because of their function, portolan charts generally concentrated on cities and towns along the coast; however, on Maggiolo's map many of the inland towns, such as those along the rivers of eastern Europe, are also identified by castle-like structures. The attention given to these towns indicates their recognized position as centers of cultural, political, and industrial life. Like many other mapmakers of this period, Maggiolo was apparently not very familiar with the architectural styles of Africa and Asia; he simply transferred the European castle to foreign soil. On at least one sixteenth-century map, the European castle was also used to represent towns in the New World.[2]

It was natural for castles to appear so often on maps, especially portolan charts, since they, like church towers and other prominent elements along the horizon, served as convenient focal points for both the makers and users of maps. An illustration from Philippe Danfrie's 1597 *Treatise on the Usage of Trigonometry* (fig. 20) shows a surveyor taking his sights on a castle tower on a hill. With their tall towers and, usually, elevated locations, castles also gave mapmakers the opportunity to get an overall view of the surrounding area. In July 1576, for instance, Queen Elizabeth ordered all town officials in Wales to assist the mapmaker Christopher Saxton by seeing him "conducted unto any towre Castle highe place or hill to view that country."[3] The maps that resulted from Saxton's survey make up the earliest national atlas, first published in 1579. On these engraved maps, Saxton used a conventional symbol, a tower motif, to mark off the many castles of the British Isles.

Some of the most specific renderings of castles appear on the cartographic views and plans of the sixteenth and seventeenth centuries. Of particular interest are those that make up the *Civitates orbis terrarum (Towns of the World)*, a six-volume atlas published between 1572 and 1618 by Georg Braun and Frans Hogenberg. Their view of the town of Sion (Sitten) from the first volume shows an extremely detailed rendering of the picturesque Swiss city built around two prominent hills (fig. 21). The drawing for this bird's-eye view appears to have been made from the top of a neighboring mountain. On the height to the north (left) stands the bishop's castle of Tourbillon erected in 1294, here identified as the *Fürstlich Schloss* (the prince's palace). On the lower hill, to the right, is the castle of Valeria, which includes the thirteenth-century church of

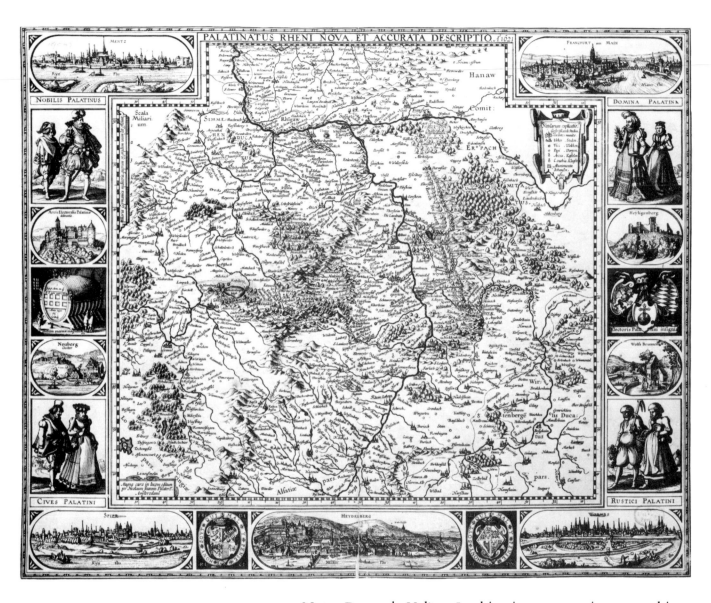

22

Map of the Rhineland Palatinate.
Claes Jansz. Visscher, 1621.
Courtesy of Staatsbibliothek
Preussischer Kulturbesitz, Berlin

Notre Dame de Valère. In this picturesque view everything that the early mapmakers presented in symbolic or summary fashion — castles, walls of fortification, and all the buildings in between — is spelled out in loving detail. Unlike the rest of the town, which is viewed from above, the castles, because of their extreme elevation, are seen at or above eye level. Beautifully silhouetted against the sky, the two medieval structures are prominent local landmarks. As in the majority of the maps discussed so far, the castle continues to symbolize the town.

As maps became more scientific, many of the pictorial elements were replaced by conventional symbols. Signs

23
Detail: Map of Hampshire.
Isaac Taylor, 1759.
Photograph courtesy of
the Houghton Library,
Harvard University

used to indicate the castle ranged from simplified designs like those first seen on Matthew Paris's map (fig. 16) to more abstract forms like circles or dots. Fortunately, the greater detail and accuracy that began to appear in mapmaking in the sixteenth century did not mean the complete elimination of ornamentation. In fact, the maps of the seventeenth century are among the most decorative in the history of cartography.

To compensate for the lack of space on the maps themselves, mapmakers often added decorative borders around the sides. This is the case in Claes Jansz. Visscher's engraved folio-size map of a region rich in castles, the Rhineland Palatinate (fig. 22). First issued in 1621, this Dutch map uses a common cartographic symbol, a circle with a flag, to mark off the many castles in the area. The outside border includes figures, coats of arms, and views of towns and castles. The most important castle of the region, Heidelberg, appears twice: in the view of the town at the bottom and in a separate rendering at the upper left. On the right side is a view of another castle Heÿligenberg. These two German landmarks, which symbolize power and nobility, are appropriately displayed below figures who represent the aristocracy.

Considering the eighteenth century's renewed interest in the Middle Ages, it is not surprising to find mapmakers of this period continuing to work with castle imagery. Isaac Taylor's engraved wall map of Hampshire county, dated 1759, includes views of three castles. Like those on the Visscher map, they are separated from the map itself, this time by ornate rococo frames. In two of the views, those of Portchester and Carisbrooke (fig. 23), delicately etched scenes of castles in remote and idyllic settings suggest the romanticism that the modern world associated with antique structures. Fascination with old castles and how they changed over the years is even further indicated by Taylor's symbol for "Castles demolish'd" — two truncated towers. Thus, by the eighteenth century, the castle was no longer primarily a symbol of power and activity, but a reminder of the past.

As these examples show, the castle motif played an important role in mapmaking for a period of well over five hundred years. From medieval depictions stressing the castle's functional role to the much later, romanticized versions representing times past, castles on maps document the symbolism of these structures and how it changed over the years.

Naomi Reed Kline
The Gothic Revival

The Middle Ages were followed by the Renaissance, a time when there was a rebirth of interest in the Classical ideals of ancient Greece and Rome. For approximately three hundred years (roughly 1500-1800), Europe continued to absorb the influence of Renaissance styles; and although the Renaissance has been described as a period without sympathy for the Middle Ages, castle-like buildings continued to be built, albeit in the more domestic guise of castellated manor houses and châteaux. "Even where the peace was fairly secure, the penchant of lately ennobled families at all periods to lay claim to chivalric origins, and thus to assert their kinship with the great, served to perpetuate the old motives but little altered."[1]

Although this was particularly true of France, architecture in England at the advent of the Reformation dissociated itself, to a large extent, from the military ethos of the castle. Once centers of feudal power and economic activity, military fortifications were either ignored as belonging to an earlier, more primitive time, or attacked as symbols of an abhorrent religious and feudal order. The broken silhouettes of medieval castles came to be seen as worthless remains of the thousand years of European history that followed the fall of Rome in the year 410. The English referred pejoratively to this entire era as the "Gothick," as our word Gothic was then spelled, after the tribal marauders of Roman times.

Cultural survivals of the Middle Ages had been maligned as barbarian or backward, partly because they were considered provincial in the context of the Renaissance view of a broader, more coherent Western intellectual and artistic tradition. Still, the potential for a renewed appreciation of castle and cathedral was present, especially as ideas of nationalism grew. And by the late eighteenth century, attitudes began to change accordingly.

First scholars and amateurs, and then a wider segment of the public, became interested in medieval art and architecture and, eventually, in the texture of life in the Middle Ages. Much of their interest focused on the ruined castles and abbeys that dotted the European landscape, the most tangible link between the eighteenth century and the medieval world. Enthusiasm for the medieval — a phenomenon known as the "Gothic Revival" — first appeared in England, though it was later embraced in other countries. Its influence was strongest in the disciplines of architecture and literature.

This revival of interest, when it came, emerged from the tranquility of the libraries and studies of leisured English scholars who approached the Gothic, in the form of ruined monuments, with the precision of antiquarians. The architectural relics of the Middle Ages — cathedrals and castles — were carefully catalogued and described as curiosities of interest. No longer considered threatening as military bastions, castles became objects of art, resuscitated with pen, ink, and the copper engraving plate.

Large, lavishly illustrated books recording architectural antiquities appeared in costly limited editions for the private libraries of people of means. In England by the late eighteenth century, Thomas Hearne, Francis Grose, Henry Boswell, and the Buck brothers — to mention only a few — described the silent architectural remains of an age once filled with bustling life (fig. 24). Such scholarly volumes were followed by a growing number of journals published by local historical societies. Articles of antiquarian appeal also began to fill the pages of the appropriately titled Gentlemen's Magazine. For the general populace, this surge of pedantic interest was translated into more accessible and inexpensive travel guides.

A taste for the medieval evolved. It was a taste that in part reflected an interest in historical and genealogical associations, but it also selectively ordered the world into a picturesque mold. Unlike the balance and symmetry of the Classical style, the irregularity of Gothic buildings found appreciation once again and was juxtaposed with natural landscapes by painters and draftsmen. If one could not build a small sham castle (a constructed ruin) in the garden as a permanent fixture for one's reveries, one could visit the countryside, guidebook in hand, and happen upon the ruins of more genuine castles. A new — and self-conscious — way of seeing thus became fashionable.

In literature, at about this time, a group of writers known as the graveyard poets began to publish works reflecting the prevailing taste for the Gothic. Graveyards, abbeys, ruined churches, and abandoned castles offered the necessary ingredients for the melancholy scenarios of these writers. Crumbling, moldering medieval buildings were regarded as evidence of a time past and as reminders of the fleeting present, as in Payne Knight's poetry.

Through to the clouds his castle seemed to climb
And frown'd defiance to the desperate foe,
Though deem'd invincible, the conqueror,
Time levell'd the fabric, as the founder, low.[2]

The poet Thomas Gray, also a distinguished archaeologist,

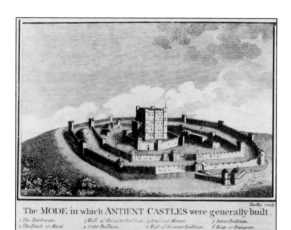

24

Illustration from Boswell and Baum,
Historical Description of New
and Elegant Views of the Antiquities
of England and Wales, *1783.*
*Courtesy of the Houghton
Library, Harvard University*

exemplified this pleasurably gloomy strain along with Robert Blair (The Grave, *1743), Edward Young* (Night Thoughts, *1742-1745), and Thomas Warton ("The Pleasure of Melancholy," 1747), among others. Gray is best known for his "Elegy Written in a Country Churchyard" (1751).*

  The taste for the medieval — if not for the gloomy — inspired both domestic architecture and works of fiction. In 1747, Horace Walpole, a collector and writer, established himself at the small villa called Strawberry Hill. Soon afterwards he reconstructed it in the Gothic style and, by making substantial additions to the building, created his own grandiose version of the sham castle (figs. 25, 26). Strawberry Hill, dubbed a major monument of "rococo gothic" by Kenneth Clark, was more a monument to Walpole's imagination than a replica of an actual castle. It incorporated plaster fan vaults and battlements of wood, of which Walpole wrote: "Every true Goth must perceive that [my rooms] are more the work of fancy than imitation." An eclectic creation, inspired by bits and pieces of Gothic monuments recorded in antiquarian tomes, Strawberry Hill heralded a transition from the facts of the antiquarians to the fancy of the Gothic Revivalists.

26
Illustration:
Library at Strawberry Hill, from
1A Description of the Villa of
Mr. Horace Walpole.
Courtesy of the Lewis Walpole Library,
Yale University,
Farmington, Connecticut

According to Walpole, the neo-Gothic Strawberry Hill provided the inspiration for his Castle of Otranto *(1764), often cited as the first Gothic novel — a genre that was in a sense the successor of the works of the graveyard poets. In this book Walpole gave architecture a prominence it had not hitherto enjoyed in the English novel. As backdrop for the narrative, the castle was given a central role in the plot; haunted towers, trap doors, and great stairways provided the characters with an atmosphere of suspense and intrigue and heightened the novel's sublime effects.*

The sublime, an aesthetic concept like the picturesque, had been defined by Edmund Burke in A Philosophical Enquiry into the Origin of Our Ideas of the Sublime and Beautiful *"Whatever is fitted in any sort to excite the ideas of pain and danger," Burke wrote, "that is to say, whatever is in any sort terrible, or is conversant about terrible objects, or operates in a manner analagous to terror, is a source of the sublime."[4] In other words things sublime had an overwhelming effect upon the beholder, arousing fear and awe. Unlike the pleasing effect of the picturesque, the sublime inspired a sense of mystery and gloom akin to a sentimental melancholy.*

William Beckford (1760-1844), who also tried his hand at the Gothic novel, followed Walpole by building Fonthill Abbey, another Gothic residence (fig. 27). Fonthill Abbey, however, was more in keeping with Walpole's Castle of Otranto, *the literary fiction, than with Strawberry Hill, the architecture of which was more picturesque than sublime. With its awe-inspiring verticality, Fonthill Abbey was a monument to the sublime in which dramatic effects were paramount.*

There was little concern for authenticity (this supposed abbey contained a castle's great hall) or for structural soundness in Beckford's abbey. The 276-foot-high great tower which crowned this extraordinary building collapsed during Beckford's lifetime; in the haste of construction, the contractor had apparently failed to support the structure with a suitable foundation. That Fonthill lacked an adequate foundation underscores the simultaneously whimsical and grandiose nature of this and other eighteenth-century undertakings, so far removed from the structural concerns of true medieval style.

Walpole and Beckford led the way for a new generation of Gothic novelists, such as Charlotte Smith (1749-1806) and Ann Radcliffe (1764-1823), who built castles of words as a kind of operatic stage-set for their sublime and convoluted tales of the horrific. In The Mysteries of Udolpho *(1794), Mrs. Radcliffe, perhaps the most popular of Gothic novelists, describes the "silent, lonely, and sublime" Castle of Udolpho:[5]*

The gateway before her, leading into the courts, was of gigantic size and defended by two round towers, crowned by overhanging turrets, embattled, where instead of banners, now waved long grass and wild plants, that had taken root among the mouldering stones and which seemed to sigh, as the breeze rolled past, over the desolation around them.[6]

In the following essay, The Castle in the Gothic Novel, *Robin Feuer Miller explores the significance of the castle in the work of the Gothic novelists.*

The Romantic undercurrent emerging in fiction and poetry also inspired attempts to revive authentic medieval works. Gray edited Welsh and Norse poetry, while Thomas Percy's Reliques of Ancient English Poetry *(1765) brought English ballads to light. James Macpherson's so-called translations of the work of a third-century Gaelic poet named Ossian, although eventually shown to be forgeries, also enjoyed enormous popularity.*

But it was the novels of Sir Walter Scott that finally gave a more accurate historical foundation to the romance of castles. As Leslie J. Workman points out in his essay, To Castle Dangerous: The Influence of Scott, *Scott combined an antiquarian's knowledge with the ability to write lively, palatable history. Unlike the Gothic novelists, whose understanding of medieval life and manners was largely gleaned from Shakespeare, Scott carefully researched his tales and visited the sites of his stories in order to reproduce them faithfully in words. His books became extremely popular and, by the early decades of the nineteenth century, they were widely read and disseminated.*

The illustration of Scott's works became an occupation in itself. An army of artists, including J.M.W. Turner, traversed the British countryside in order to capture the landmarks and locales of Waverly *and* Ivanhoe. *By the mid-nineteenth century, as Martin Krause points out in his essay* From Antiquarian to Romantic: The Castle Illustrated, *the exacting topographical studies characteristic of the earlier antiquarian tomes had been replaced by the atmospheric landscapes of Romantic illustration.*

Americans of the early 1800s still relied largely on the English to establish the fashions of cultural life, and Romanticism in its many forms ultimately found an eager audience in the United States. By the first decade of the century the American author Washington Irving and his friend, Washington Allston, had visited Europe and returned to America to translate Romanticism into their respective idioms. Clearly, they were strongly influenced by the literature of the Gothic Revival. On Irving's arrival in France in 1804, he wrote this note about a castle in his journal: "It had a most picturesque appearance as the first glimpse of morning fell on its mouldering towers. It

27
Engraving:
Fonthill Abbey, from
Delineations of Fonthill and its Abbey,
by John Rutter, 1823.
Courtesy of Hammond Castle Museum Library,
Gloucester, Massachusetts

28
Oil on canvas: An Italian Autumn.
Thomas Cole, 1844.
Courtesy of the Walker Art Center, Minneapolis;
Gift of the T.B. Walker Foundation

stood on the brow of a high bank of the river which glittered at its base. The description of Mrs. Radcliffe was brought immediately to my recollection."[7]

If Mrs. Radcliffe influenced the generation of Allston and Irving, Scott's works were to have an even greater impact upon the next generation of American painters, architects, and writers. In the field of painting, several artists who intermittently found inspiration in the upstate New York landscape (and were therefore later called members of the Hudson River School) traveled to Europe where they steeped themselves in European Romanticism. Artists such as Thomas Cole (1801-1848), Jasper F. Cropsey (1823-1900), Asher Durand (1796-1886), and Sanford Robinson Gifford (1823-1880) returned to America with fresh visions and an awakened sensitivity to the American countryside. Typically they glorified the grander aspects of nature. As Ellwood C. Parry points out in his essay, Towers Above the Trees in Romantic Landscape Paintings, *they relied on memory, sometimes refreshed by their own sketches or English illustrated volumes, to paint real or imaginary buildings in their historical landscape paintings as a theme-enhancing backdrop, rich in associations (fig. 28).*

While the artists painted, architects were busy at work punctuating the Hudson River Valley with real castles of stone and mortar. By mid-century the Hudson began to resemble the Rhine as much in architecture as in topography. The imagined world of the medieval revival had begun to impose its own image on the American landscape.

Robin Feuer Miller *The Castle in the Gothic Novel*

Ever since its pinnacles were first glimpsed through the rays of the setting sun or through a sudden lifting of the fog, the fictional Gothic castle has provoked in character and reader alike a pleasurable sensation of intermingled dread and anticipation. The evocation of the "pleasantly terrifying" emotion forms the bedrock of the Gothic novel or tale of terror, as it is frequently called. It provides the common denominator among the works of such diverse writers as Horace Walpole, Ann Radcliffe, Matthew G. Lewis, and Charles Maturin. Another name for what provokes this response is, of course, the sublime.

In a *Philosophical Enquiry into the Origin of Our Ideas of the Sublime and Beautiful*, Edmund Burke defined the sublime as that which excites "the ideas of pain and danger . . . whatever is in any sort terrible, or is conversant about terrible objects, or operates in a manner analagous to terror." Burke distinguished the beautiful from the sublime: one fills us with pleasure, the other with delight. The beautiful induces "in us a sense of affection and tenderness," but the sublime "is productive of the strongest emotion which the mind is capable of feeling."[1]

The Gothic novelists of the late eighteenth and early nineteenth century, described a world in which the sublime and the beautiful were tightly entangled, where the beautiful was encroached upon by terror, surrounded by and merged with horror. In Mario Praz's words, "The discovery of Horror as a source of delight reacted in men's actual conception of Beauty itself: the Horrid, from being a category of the Beautiful becomes eventually one of its essential elements, and the 'beautifully horrid' passed by insensible degrees into the 'horribly beautiful'."[2]

Most often the site chosen for this depiction of the uncanny and the dreadful was the castle. In the first Gothic novel, Horace Walpole's *The Castle of Otranto* (1764), the gloomy castle with its subterranean vaults is simultaneously the theater of action, the prison of the heroine and the hero, and a metaphoric extension of its owner, the hero-villain Manfred (fig. 29). Indeed the castle literally falls apart when Manfred's ruin comes to pass. Likewise the castle in Ann Radcliffe's *The Mysteries of*

Udolpho (1794) becomes a metaphoric equivalent to its evil possessor, Montoni, who imprisons the virtuous Emily within its walls.

The castle and, likewise, the ruined castle, the cathedral, and the abbey offered the Gothic novelist as rich an opportunity for creating an atmosphere of mystery, wildness, and danger — in short, the sublime — as could any mountain, waterfall, or blasted heath. Even better, the Gothic castle could symbolize the intermingling of art and nature, for it affected people in the same way as did the most grandiose of natural phenomena. Yet it was man-made, an artificial creation, a concrete edifice in the real world and at the same time a powerful symbol for the imaginary, even unconscious, landscapes of the human mind. In fact, the very genre of the Gothic novel was born of Walpole's dream of a castle. "Shall I confess to you," he wrote to a friend, "what was the origin of this romance? I waked one morning in the beginning of last June from a dream, of which all I could recover was, that I had thought myself in an ancient castle . . . and that, on the uppermost banister of a great staircase, I saw a gigantic hand in armour. In the evening I sat down and began to write, without knowing in the least what I intended to say or relate."[3]

Aside from the evocation of the sublime, perhaps the most compelling similarity in the ways the castle and the mountain or ocean (the grandiose) affect the spectator is through the arousal of the imagination. Classical architecture, as one critic has observed, was "flooded with light, leaving nothing to the imagination, but Gothic architecture was filled with impenetrable shadows and mysterious vistas, which might conceal anything of an exciting nature. The ends of great halls and chapels, and the roofs of high-vaulted rooms were often lost in darkness."[4]

Paradoxically, the castle of Gothic fiction, which functions as a symbol of a character's submission to his unconscious impulses and to the world of the unfettered, free imagination, was a consciously wrought image, carefully created by novelists who knew precisely what effect they hoped to achieve. The rise of the Gothic novel or tale of terror paralleled the new value placed on sensibility — the capacity for refined emotion, the readiness to feel compassion for suffering and to be moved by the pathetic in literature, art, and life.

The ruined castle, suggestive of the transience of human

29

Frontispiece: Castle of Otranto,
by Horace Walpole, 1796.
Courtesy of the Houghton Library,
Harvard University

existence, gave the Gothic novelist and her (or, less often, his) heroines both a melancholy inspiration and a suitable atmosphere for reverie. One heroine muses, "I doat on ruins; there is something sublime and awful in the sight of decayed grandeur and large edifices tumbling to pieces." And the heroine in another novel observes that the peaked roof of a castle, "half lost in air, and half, by straining her sight, kept in view, excited mingled passions — a sensation of terror and delight." Similarly, such constructions made Charles Maturin "tremble with a delicious dread," for they presented "that mixture of deviation and decay that combines our admiration of greatness with our interest in debility."[5]

From an architectural viewpoint, the great Gothic novelists such as Ann Radcliffe or Charlotte Smith usually described their castles imprecisely. (One of the few exceptions was one Dr. Nathan Drake, a little-known writer whose *Literary Hours* (1800) employs such sophisticated and accurate architectural terminology as "barbican" and "outer and inner ballium.") Instead, the importance of the castle for these writers lay in its power to evoke an emotional, psychological, and atmospheric response — an aim with which all of the Gothic novelists were obsessed.

Despite their ignorance about the actual physical properties of the castle, the Gothic novelists played a significant role in awakening the interest of the public in architecture. Warren Hunt Smith has described this process:

The effect of these novels has been to inculcate architectural prejudices, to invest certain styles and buildings with a glamour quite independent of their physical structure, to reclothe historic edifices with the apparel of their vanished youth, and even to revive past styles of design. In such ways, English fiction has been unusually effective, and a knowledge of architecture as popularized in the novel is essential for a thorough understanding of English architectural history.[6]

But the novelists of the late eighteenth and nineteenth centuries quickly became aware of the colossal cliché they had erected in constructing their fictional castles. Charlotte Smith, for example, who began her career as one of the first and most sincere Gothic novelists, and whose works were generously laden with mysterious castles, ended by parodying the expectations aroused by those same edifices. In *The Banished Man* (1794) she writes, "Be not alarmed, gentle reader, though seven castles shall have been talked of in a preface, thou shalt not be compelled to enter on another at this late period of the story . . . the wallflower and the fern shall not nod over the broken battlements, nor shall the eastern tower or any tower, be enwreathed with the mantling ivy." And in *The Young Philosopher*" (1798), one of her characters says: "It [the tapestry] was nailed down so that I could not move it, nor could the wind perform any of those operations upon it which constitute great part of the terror in some novels."

An even more extreme satiric portrayal of the Gothic castle is found in T.J. Horsley Curties's *Scottish Legend* (1802), where a concealed passage in a castle "descending into the vaults, winds for miles under the country," and the same castle is said "to rival even the ages themselves in altitude and greatness." Charles Dickens, though by no means a Gothic novelist, gives us in *Great Expectations* (1860-1861) a gentler, humorous version of a Gothic castle in the form of Wemmick's little wooden cottage. The top "was cut out and painted like a battery mounted with guns." Although it was the smallest house Pip had ever seen, it had "the queerest gothic windows (by far the greater part of them sham), and a gothic door, almost too small to get in at." The castle even possesses a moat — "a chasm about four feet wide and two deep" — and "the bridge was a plank... But it was very pleasant to see the pride with which he [Wemmick] hoisted it up." Pip sleeps, appropriately, in a little "turret bedroom."

Indeed, the titles of the parodies of the Gothic novel which were emerging at the same time as the novels themselves further emphasize the crucial role of the castle — Jane Austen's *Northanger Abbey* (1803, published in 1818), for instance, or Thomas Love Peacock's *Headlong Hall* (1816) and *Nightmare Abbey* (1818). Even a straightforward list of the titles of Gothic novels reveals the importance of the castle or abbey. In a listing of approximately 320 such novels, eighty–five contained references to a castle or abbey in the title, such as *The Castle of Wolfenbach, Craig Melrose Abbey, Bungay Castle, Count Roderic's Castle, Edgar or the Phantom of the Castle,* and *The Horrors of Oakendale Abbey.*

Despite the many parodies of the Gothic novel and its gloomy castles, and despite the proliferation since the late eighteenth century of third- and fourth-rate dimestore versions of these works (evident in the hugely successful "gothic romances" that provide the bread and butter for so many publishing houses today), writers and critics have continued to find the literary Gothic castle a rich source of inspiration.

As critics attempt to characterize the genre of the Gothic novel, they inevitably cite the depiction of the castle or abbey as one of its identifying marks. In fact, Eino Railo, one of the foremost students of the Gothic novel, goes so far as to make the haunted castle the crucial defining indicator of the Gothic novel. "The reader," he writes, "quickly observes that this 'haunted castle' plays an exceedingly important part in these romances; so important, indeed, that were it eliminated, the whole fabric of romance would be bereft of its foundation and would lose its predominant atmosphere. The entire stock-in-trade of horror-romanticism in its oldest and purest form consists... chiefly of the properties and stuff of this haunted castle."[7] His monumental work on the Gothic novel is entitled, simply, *The Haunted Castle.*

Devendra P. Varma has interpreted the Gothic novelists' preoccupation with the castle as an indirect rebellion against the beginnings of the industrial revolution and as a metaphor for the grave anxiety produced by the economic and social changes of the late eighteenth and early nineteenth centuries. "The Gothic romance, with its ruined abbeys, frowning castle, haunted galleries, and feudal halls, its pathless forests and lonely landscapes, records a revolt against the oppressive materialism of the time." Coupled with their dread of the future, however, was the Gothic novelists' consciousness of the "decadence of the old order." Thus the ruined Gothic castle and the phantoms wandering its corridors also symbolized "the inexplicable fear of the return of bygone powers.[8]

In general, however, interpretations of the role of Gothic architecture in fiction seem to fall into two camps. Some critics see it as providing a backdrop, a profoundly suggestive atmosphere for the events of the story, while others discover in Gothic architecture a physical embodiment of the psyche, a symbol capable of expressing and reflecting the full range of human consciousness and unconsciousness (fig. 30).

For the first group, the labyrinths, catacombs, and dark passages of the Gothic cathedral or castle enhance the effects of the melodramatic plots the Gothic novelists were so fond of. Thus G.R. Thompson writes that Walpole, the first Gothic novelist, was able "by emphasizing the vaults, stained windows, tombs, darkness and carefully coordinated perspective of medieval buildings" to effect "a shift of meaning in the most common use of the word *Gothic* from the architectural denotation of 'Medieval buildings' to the emotional effect of weird, supernatural, fantastic, and terrifying events in a work of literature in which the Medieval cathedral or castle served as a theater for such events."[9] James Keech finds similarities between William Faulkner's ruined Southern antebellum mansions and the Gothic castle or haunted abbey — their atmosphere of romantic decay, their evocation of vanished glory, their associations with "latent horror, a kind of Gothic curse."[10]

The second group of critics find the response to Gothic architecture so powerful that it no longer simply provides the atmosphere but rather merges with and symbolizes the self. The pattern for this mode of response was set by the contemporaries of the Gothic novelists. Samuel Taylor Coleridge wrote, for example, in *General Character of the Gothic Literature and Art:*
The Greek art is beautiful, when I enter a Greek church, my eye is charmed, and my mind elated; I feel exalted and proud that I am a man. But the Gothic art is sublime. On entering a cathedral, I am filled with devotion and with awe; I am lost to the actualities that surround me, and my whole being expands into the infinite; earth and air, nature and art, all swell up into eternity, and the only sensible impression left is 'that I am nothing!'[11]

30
Frontispiece: The Monk,
by Matthew Lewis, ca. 1820.
Courtesy of the Houghton Library,
Harvard University

A modern critic, Joel Porte, welds the roles of Gothic architecture as backdrop and as symbol: "It provided par excellence that dim religious atmosphere where the union of Terror and Sublimity which was alone considered capable of transporting the soul beyond reason and decorum to the very confines of Being itself could be achieved."[12]

For some, the psychological function of the castle in the Gothic novel may be a Jungian one. The heroine in a Gothic novel may find her feminine sensibilities attacked by the "masculine" presence of a castle. Thus of Mrs. Radcliffe's *Mysteries of Udolpho,* Barton Levi St. Armand writes that Emily's "mediumistic powers of revery and feminine weaving of the warp of landscape with the woof of dreamscape are halted only by a traumatic confrontation with the dark and limiting male reality of Udolpho [the castle] itself... From a conveniently modern Jungian perspective, we could say that the Anima has here met the Shadow."[13]

For others the role of the castle is, instead, best described in Freudian terms, interlaced with an eclectic appropriation of any other psychological terminology that seems handy. Leslie Fiedler, for instance, believes the castle suggests a map of the human psyche:

Beneath the haunted castle lies the dungeon keep: the womb from whose darkness the ego first emerged, the tomb to which it knows it must return at last. Beneath the crumbling shell of paternal authority, lies the maternal blackness, imagined by the gothic writer as a prison, a torture chamber — from which the cries of the kidnapped *anima* cannot even be heard. The upper and the lower levels of the ruined castle or abbey represent the contradictory fears at the heart of gothic terror: the dread of the super-ego, whose splendid battlements have been battered but not quite cast down — and of the id, whose buried darkness abounds in dark visions no stormer of the castle had even touched.[14]

Whatever finally seems the best explanation of its function in the Gothic novel, the castle has evoked a powerful — even magical — response in most readers. It comes as no surprise that first editions of the Gothic novels are extremely rare; they were literally reduced to shreds from use. Sir Walter Scott wrote of the rage for *The Mysteries of Udolpho,* "The volumes flew and were sometimes torn from hand to hand."

The Gothic novelists, whether they were depicting the quest for the numinous, the presence of all-pervading evil, an atmosphere fraught with appalling tension, or a virtuous maiden in distress, never lost sight of the specific response they were trying to provoke in their readers. The Gothic novel may have the been the "leaf-mould" in which "more exquisite and stronger plants" of Romanticism took root, or it may have provided "Romanticism with its first full set of swaddling clothes."[15] But it cannot be viewed simply as the precursor of Romanticism. Its authors were undisputed masters at holding their readers' attention and deserve our own.

Coleridge wrote in his review of *The Mysteries of Udolpho* that "curiosity is a kind of appetite, and hurries headlong on, impatient for its complete gratification." Scott, reviewing the same novel, observed that "it is not until the last page is read . . . that we feel ourselves disposed to censure that which has so keenly interested us." The curiosity and keen interest which Coleridge and Scott have described were inspired and tantalized in large measure by the fictional Gothic castle.

31

Engraving: "Dryburgh Abbey, the resting place of Sir Walter Scott," from Castle Dangerous, *by Sir Walter Scott. From an 1887 edition*

Leslie J. Workman

To Castle Dangerous:
The Influence
of Scott

When Sir Walter Scott died in November 1832, he was mourned around the world (fig. 31). At a public meeting in Albany, New York, Harmanus Bleecker observed with justice that "the writings of Walter Scott are familiar to dwellers on the banks of the Ganges and the Mississippi." The *Ontario Repository* reported honors paid in a remote village at the "Waverly Rock." American newspapers edged their columns in black, and paragraphs on Scott continued to appear into the New Year.

The reaction to Scott's death was in keeping with his enormous popularity throughout his career. His first major poem, *The Lay of the Last Minstrel* (1805), sold 15,000 copies in five years. As Scott's best and most recent biographer, Edgar Johnson, points out, "In a period when the total population of England and Scotland was fewer than twelve million, and the bare ability to read was far from being a general accomplishment, such sales were a spectacular triumph."[1] *Waverly* (1814), Scott's first novel, sold 5,000 copies in the first year, a record for an anonymous novel. When it was reprinted in 1829 as part of the *Magnum Opus* (a reissue of all Scott's novels with new prefaces), never having been out of print, *Waverly* sold 25,000 copies in a few days. "All former bookselling is a joke to this," said Robert Cadell, the publisher.

These figures do not include the vast sales of both authorized and pirated editions outside Great Britain. In the United States enterprising publishers paid large sums for stolen proof sheets, distributed them to several printers for almost overnight printing, and rushed the results to booksellers in special coaches.

Scott's poems and novels, coinciding with the Romantic interest in "sublime" scenery and historic places (fig. 32), preferably ruined, and the development of the railroad and the steamboat, virtually created the tourist industry in Scotland. Parisian fashion discovered the tartan and the tweed. Scottish history, scenery, and legend became the themes of paintings, books, and orchestral works — those of Mendelssohn and Bruch are only the best known examples. Donizetti's *Lucia di Lammermoor* (1835) is one of the three operas and twenty known dramatic treatments

32
Engraving: Windsor, from Woodstock,
*by Sir Walter Scott.
From an 1887 edition*

of Scott's *Bride of Lammermoor* (1819). *Ivanhoe* (1820) inspired twenty-nine stage versions. Altogether there are more than 250 theatrical versions of Scott's poems and novels, not counting films, and more than three dozen operas. Today Scott retains his popularity to a surprising degree at the box office, in public libraries, and in the paperback book market. Perhaps the simplest way to measure Scott's impact is to consider the case of Wales and Ireland, both of which had quite as much as Scotland to offer the Romantic tourist, artist, or historian. All they lacked was a genius like Scott to bring them to popular attention.

Scott's success depended on three elements, combined for the first time in his work. One was the approach and equipment of the realist–novelist; like his predecessors, Fielding and Smollett, Scott drew on an extensive experience of men and affairs, as landowner, lawyer, public official, editor, publisher, and even economist. The second element was a powerful imagination nourished not only on the living tradition of the Border ballads but on the drama and atmosphere of Gothic romance. Scott grew up in a Border society still close to its feudal and heroic past as well as to the flourishing commercial and intellectual life of Edinburgh. This juxtaposition of ancient and modern gave Scott a vital key to the nature of the historical process. The third factor was Scott's vast antiquarian and historical knowledge which his prodigious memory enabled him to use easily and naturally. The result was "for the first time in either fiction *or* history . . . to dramatise the basic processes of history."[2]

33

Engraving: "Day set upon Norham's castled steep,"
from "Marmion,"
by Sir Walter Scott.
From an 1864 edition

34

Engraving: "Old Barnard's towers are purple still,"
from "Rokeby," by Sir Walter Scott.
From an 1864 edition

The eighteenth century had made great advances in the theory of history: Hegel had given it a philosophy and Voltaire a method. Edward Gibbon, in *The Decline and Fall of the Roman Empire* (1776-1788), had shown what could be done with the existing science of history. But Gibbon's history, as G.M. Trevelyan remarked, was "like the procession in the Parthenon frieze," a procession of eighteenth-century gentlemen in costume.[3]

Scott showed how thought and behavior are changed by time, place, and circumstance. This synthesizing imagination was the key to the great outburst of historical writing in the nineteenth century. "The difference between Gibbon and Macaulay," said Trevelyan, "is a measure of the influence of Scott." Thomas Babington Macaulay's *History of England* (1848-1861) was, significantly, the first work to outsell *The Lay of the Last Minstrel.*

The frontier for the nineteenth-century historian was the largely unknown Middle Ages, which Scott had shown as equal in importance to the Classical world. If Scott had such a great impact on the educated view of the past, his enormous effect on the popular imagination was to be expected. Every novel revealed a new and previously unknown era to a public hungry for sensation. Yet even this might not explain Scott's influence, were there not more powerful motives for turning to the Middle Ages in both Europe and America.

The English preferred to attribute the power and prosperity of the early nineteenth century not so much to the Industrial Revolution as to the long and pragmatic development of English institutions: "Old England" had long been their favorite way of referring to their country. In France opposite causes produced a like effect: the loss of political direction following the overthrow of Napoleon, a half-century of political experiments punctuated by revolution, could only be reconciled with national pride by taking a longer view. The historian Jules Michelet called on his countrymen to think in terms of "the epic of the people" through past ages. Germany had emerged from the Napoleonic era vigorous but still divided into more than thirty separate states. Many felt that political unity could only come as a result of a sense of identity that would be the product of recalling the past achievements of German culture. This inspired, for example, the life work of Jacob and Wilhelm Grimm in language and mythology, of which the fairy tales *(Kinder-und Hausmärchen,* 1812-1822) were a by-product.

35
*Engraving: Warwick Castle,
Moonlight View, from* Kenilworth,
*by Sir Walter Scott.
From an 1887 edition*

36
*Engraving: Round Tower, Windsor, 1660,
from* Woodstock, *by Sir Walter Scott.
From an 1887 edition*

If medievalism itself, the rejection in half a century of the Classical model that had dominated Europe for fifteen hundred years, is a surprising phenomenon, American medievalism is at first glance its most surprising feature — since the American Revolution, though less explicitly than the French, had involved a rejection of feudalism. But the common medieval past was equally necessary to Europe and America. Lacking the physical remains of the Middle Ages, nothing was more natural to Americans than, with characteristic energy, to set about supplying them — especially since, as both Scott and the American architect Andrew Jackson Downing, pointed out, the Gothic style was better suited to the northern climate and scene than the Classical.

The lack of physical remains in the New World meant, however, that most Americans got their knowledge of the Middle Ages from reading, which meant primarily, if not excusively, from Scott. This factor lends some color to the theory (to which Mark Twain with less than his usual felicity devoted a chapter of *Life on the Mississippi*) that "Sir Walter Scott had so large a hand in making Southern character as it existed before the war, that he is in great measure responsible for the war." Twain, who also attacked Gothic Revival architecture, may be forgiven for not knowing that the Gothic was a continuous tradition, even in America. But he was wrong about the Middle Ages and, in this case, wrong about his countrymen. People in the North read Scott, too. Twain's words make it difficult to believe that he had ever read a word of Scott, who was certainly the last person to idealize chivalry, as Twain declared. *Ivanhoe*, an essay on the futility of chivalry, casts a merciless spotlight on the "brilliant but useless" King Richard Lionheart. What Twain's remarks show is the pervasive influence of Scott.

The castle, virtually the symbol of Scott's influence (figs. 33, 34), and the most important prop he retained from Gothic romance, had not previously played a very important part in the English imagination, although the destruction of English castles by Parliamentary forces in the Civil War impressed folk memory enough to turn up in a popular music-hall song of the 1890s — "One of the ones that Cromwell knocked about a bit." The kind of feudal anarchy which flourished in France and Germany appeared in England only when the firm hand of the Crown relaxed, as in *Ivanhoe*. Instead, the characteristic feature of the English literary scene, from Shakespeare on, was the country house — the setting for the comedy of manners.

For castles of the imagination, the English went abroad. Children read the baroque fantasies of Perrault, such as *Cinderella, Puss in Boots,* and *The Sleeping Beauty*. Later they encountered the robber strongholds of the Grimms' fairy tales, still the typical castles for most English children today. Similarly, the castles of Gothic romance were set in the Apennines or along the Rhine.

In fact, the English word *castle* like the French *château,* had come by Scott's time to be very loosely used, referring to anything from a once fortified manor house or the peel towers of the Border, to a vast majestic pile like Caernarvon or Warwick (fig. 35). This helped to open the way for the castellated style in architecture, exemplified by the Scottish Baronial homes inspired by Scott's own Abbotsford, and the American-built towers intended to make the Hudson look more like the Rhine, or by the kind of public buildings that so irritated Mark Twain.

In the late eighteenth century, however, location or place began to assume a significant role in the English novel. While there are traces of this in earlier realistic fiction such as Fielding's *Tom Jones* (1749), the importance of the setting developed most strongly in the Gothic romance. Later writers took up the theme in various ways: Jane Austen parodied the Gothic in *Northanger Abbey* (1818), and in *Mansfield Park* (1814) employed the device of contrasting two country houses, a device also used by Scott in *Waverly*. In Maria Edgeworth's *Castle Rackrent* (1800) the castle, in the hands of successive owners, shows changes of time and circumstance as individuals could not. The titles of Thomas Love Peacock's satirical novels *Headlong Hall* (1816), *Nightmare Abbey* (1818), *Crochet Castle* (1831), and *Gryll Grange* (1861) reveal subtle variations in social atmosphere.

Scott himself used only four place names as the titles of books — among them the castles of *Kenilworth* (1821) and Douglas (*Castle Dangerous*, 1831), but castles appear in virtually all his works (fig. 36). The Border ballads had taught Scott the importance of place in narrative. "I like to be as minutely local as possible," he said.[4]

If Scott's subject was not set in a real place such as Kenilworth, he would borrow one. In *Woodstock* (1826), for instance, the house of the title is the actual Compton Wyniates, moved a few miles. Sometimes he took geographical liberties, as in *Quentin Durward* (1823), where

37
Watercolor: Abbotsford,
Anne Nasmyth.
Courtesy of the National
Galleries of Scotland

he used his imagination to make the setting and features of the chateau of Plessis-le-Tours reflect the character of the crafty and unscrupulous Louis XI. Scott's son-in-law and biographer, J.G. Lockhart, has described conducting the ailing Scott through the ruined castle of Douglas. Little of the castle appears in the novel, but the reader is aware that Scott could account for every step taken by his characters.

Scott also learned from the ballads not to linger over description, even when the place, like "the massive and complicated towers and walls of the old fortress of Douglas," played a central role.[5] Torquilstone in *Ivanhoe*, though its name suggests torture and oppression, is never clearly described. From the details of the siege, however, it is clear that the castle is envisaged precisely. Thus, in the words of Richard Gill, "Scott more than any other transformed the spectral castle of the Gothicists into a solid edifice rising out of the soil of a given historic place and time and weathering genuine cultural conflicts."[6]

In much the same way, Scott's own house, Abbotsford (fig. 37), the building of which engaged much of his time, marked a major change in the direction of medievalism, transforming the "Modern Gothic" of Strawberry Hill or Fonthill Abbey which Scott considered "false and foolish" into a reasonable, livable alternative to the Classical style. (Abbotsford was one of the first houses lighted by gas.) Maria Edgeworth reported, "He thinks himself entitled to spend on castle building what he earns by castle building."[7]

As a result of Scott's work, then, medievalism assumed an entirely new social importance. It was no longer simply an engaging fantasy but a means of understanding the past. Scott was not a Romantic, though his work lay at the heart of the Romantic movement. His philosophy was of the eighteenth century, reasonable and stoic; paradoxically, this made him an archetypal Romantic hero who faced success and adversity unchanged. His warmth and love of humanity informed and made possible the vast panorama he unrolled for his readers, and over all lay what C.S. Lewis has called "the air of sense." We should not forget that Balzac the realist acknowledged a debt to Scott as profound as that of Hugo the Romantic. As Edgar Johnson concluded, "No novelist of his century saw life more sanely or portrayed it more lucidly."[8]

Martin Krause *From Antiquarian to Romantic: The Castle Illustrated*

It may seem surprising that England, a self-styled nation of shopkeepers and empire builders at the threshold of its greatest century, should suddenly develop a fancy for the age of castles, knights, and chivalry. The concurrent stirrings of the Industrial Revolution and the Gothic Revival — the one looking forward, and the other backward — are difficult to reconcile at first glance. Yet a single decade witnessed Watt's steam engine (1769), Hargreave's spinning jenny (1770), Grose's *Antiquities of England and Wales* (1773), and Hearne's *Antiquities of Great Britain* (1778).

The great progressive ages have commonly expressed a nostalgic yearning for the past. But the Gothic Revival was fundamentally different from previous renascences in its preference for style over substance. What the eighteenth-century English knew about their medieval heritage was fragmentary, gleaned from snatches of legends and ballads and from surviving ruins. As the influential art and architecture critic John Ruskin wrote in *Modern Painters* (Volume 3, 1856):

All other nations have regarded their ancestors with reverence as saints and heroes; but nevertheless thought their own deeds and ways of life fitting subjects for their arts of painting or of verse. We, on the contrary, regard our ancestors as foolish and wicked, but yet find our chief artistic pleasures in descriptions of their ways of life. The Greeks and medievals honored but did not imitate their forefathers; we imitate but do not honor.

At first it was primarily scholars who shared an appreciation for the Middle Ages — expressed in the illustrated antiquarian publications that proliferated during the eighteenth century. By the last quarter of that century, engraved illustrations, of ever higher quality and complexity, began to dominate the texts. The standard for such publications appeared in 1655, when the respected antiquarian Sir William Dugdale issued the first volume of the Latin *Monasticon Anglicanum*, an illustrated record of England's pre-Reformation religious houses, whose intended audience was the Catholic gentry. By 1718 a complete edition in English was available.

Two other volumes that heightened awareness of the Gothic were Samuel and Nathaniel Buck's *Venerable*

POMFRET CASTLE in YORKSHIRE, before it was demoli

KILDEBERT LACY, having obtain'd of W.ᵐ the Norman his Countryman, a Grant of y town of Pontefract & its Demeans, built when he had dispossessed Alfric the Saxon) This Castle; which remarkable for its strength, became stain'd with the Blood of several great Men, particularly Thomas Earl of Lancaster, Leices &c. Grandson to K. Hen. 3.ᵈ who possess'd it in right of his Wife, Alice, Daughter of Hen.Lacy Earl of Lincoln, from whom, it descended to K. Hen. 4.ᵗʰ his Successors &c; also K. Rich.ᵈ 2.ᵈ Anthony Earl Rivers, Uncle to K. Edw.ᵈ 5. and S.ᵗ Rich.ᵈ Grey, brother by Mothers Side, to the said K. Edw.ᵈ 5.ᵗʰ were fatally dispatcht here. 'Twas the Castle last Surrender'd, & Demolish'd presently after the Tragedy of K. Charles the first was Perpetrated.

Sam.ᵗ Buck Sculp.ᵗ from a Drawing, taken during the Siege; now in the possession of the learned and curious Antiquary, Roger Gale Esquire.

From the original Ju worthy Friend, M.ʳ J

38
Engraving: Pomfret Castle, Yorkshire,
from A Collection of Engravings
of Castles, Abbeys, Towns, etc...,
by Nathaniel and Samuel Buck, 1711–1753.
Courtesy of the Houghton Library,
Harvard University

Remains of above 400 Castles, Monasteries, Palaces . . . (1720-1740) (fig. 38) and Francis Grose's *Antiquities of England and Wales* (1773-1787). Both were published over a period of years; their illustrations, mostly by the authors, were informative but devoid of artistic charm.

The financially successful *Antiquities of Great Britain, Illustrated in Views of Monasteries, Castles and Churches, now existing* (1778-1807) was artistically more substantial. It marked the collaboration of two noted craftsmen, Thomas Hearne, a topographical draftsman, and William Byrne, an engraver (fig. 39). Hearne traveled widely throughout Britain, making faithful renderings of ancient castles, colleges, abbeys, and other buildings. Later, in his studio, he fashioned meticulous pen-and-ink drawings as a basis for Byrne's engravings. In these drawings Hearne was apt to introduce objects he had not seen on the spot: an artfully placed tree for balance, a dramatic sky for effect, a shepherd with flock, or a flight of ravens to suggest scale. These devices had the added effect of suggesting to the viewer that a ruin was, as William Gilpin wrote in 1789, "a habitation forsaken of men and resumed by nature."[1]

The market for images of Gothic architecture was substantial at the turn of the century, and Hearne was only one of many artists who accepted commissions to record medieval antiquities, amended them slightly for effect and, in the process, helped found one of the most felicitous of art movements — the English school of landscape in watercolors. Others were Paul Sandby, Edward Dayes, Thomas Girtin, and J.M.W. Turner.

In the wake of the artists came poets, travelers, and others in search of Britain's newly revealed heritage. They were trained to see the picturesque — that is, they sought in nature the qualities that made a picture pleasing to the eye. They belonged to a growing group of Englishmen who came to be known as tourists. Gothic ruins, eroded by centuries of neglect and by the periodic ravages of man, were regarded with particular fascination. The shells of castles, abbeys, priories, and churches that littered the English countryside became points of pilgrimage for the tourist.

Touring antiquities and the wilder reaches of the Lake District, Scotland, and Wales became a popular pastime at the same time that the major volumes of engraved *Antiquities* appeared in the 1770s. During the same period, Thomas West, Thomas Pennant, and the Reverend William Gilpin began to publish their *Tours*. These

39
Engraving: Lancaster Castle,
from Antiquities of Great Britain . . .,
by Hearne and Byrne, 1786.
Courtesy of the Houghton Library,
Harvard University

guidebooks established itineraries for the traveler and provided colorful, if inaccurate, historical background on points of interest. They often went so far as to suggest exact spots from which a site could be seen to greatest advantage — that is, most picturesquely.

The theory of the picturesque, as formulated by Gilpin and others, represented one of the more eccentric by–products of English Romanticism. The term picturesque, as opposed to beautiful, was applied to objects in nature that would be pleasing in a painting: a rough, wild vista was considered more picturesque than a well–tended garden plot, a ruin more than a newly built house, a rugged oak more than a smooth beech. The work of the seventeenth-century French artist Claude Lorrain became extraordinarily popular and was considered the model of picturesque beauty. Tourists were encouraged to seek out vistas that compared favorably with his compositions. A "Claude Glass" was even available — a smoked mirror that, when placed opposite a given vista, reflected it, framed it, and softened it with a golden glow similar in effect to one of Claude's masterpieces seen through the aura of aged varnish.

Writers who celebrated the picturesque popularized such previously overlooked aspects of beauty as landscape and ruin. Their theory implied, however, that nature should be edited and even rearranged if it needed improvement. Gilpin wrote, "I am so attached to my picturesque rules, that if nature gets wrong, I cannot help putting her right."[2] Though he was speaking of his own edited drawings of nature, he was not above suggesting alterations to nature herself, and in his *Observations Relative Chiefly to Picturesque Beauty . . .* (1789), Gilpin found it proper to add a fragment of a tower to raise slightly a wall of a ruin that happened to be on one's property.

It is clear that no set of absolute rules was devised to guide the Gothic Revival. Any imagination capable of creating something from the dust of the past was given license to do so. J.M.W. Turner was one of those endowed with such an imagination.

J.M.W. Turner — later one of the most radical innovators in English watercolor and oil painting — is not usually associated with the Gothic Revival. Yet he began his career as an illustrator of Gothic subjects, and his work appeared, well into the nineteenth century, in illustrated books of antiquities and in guidebooks. Turner knew of Francis Grose and William Gilpin, whose engravings the young Turner had copied, tinted, and sold for a shilling from the window of his father's barbershop in the 1780s. He knew William Beckford, who commissioned Turner to do six views of Fonthill Abbey in 1799. And he knew Thomas Hearne and Edward Dayes, whose works served as a model for his own. Turner began his career as a topographical draftsman in the tradition of Hearne and Dayes — a profession at which he excelled. Indeed, Turner complained in 1798 that "he had more commissions than he could execute [and] got more money than he expended."[3]

From his earliest days as an artist Turner went touring.

40
Pencil on white paper:
West Front of Bath Abbey.
J.M.W. Turner, ca. 1793.
John Herron Fund, 13.439,
Indianapolis Museum of Art

41
Watercolor over pencil on white paper:
Scottish Landscape with Castle and Bridge,
J.M.W. Turner, 1801. John Herron Fund, 13.443,
Indianapolis Museum of Art

His journeys around Britain, beginning in Oxford in 1789, are recorded in his sketchbooks (fig. 40). Some of his early sketchbooks, such as those used on his tours of the Midlands in 1794 and of southern Wales in 1794, include notes as well as rough sketches of ancient sections of towns and buildings. Along with more finished drawings made on loose sheets of paper, these notations provided the information he needed to work up highly finished watercolors in his studio at a later date.

Practicality must have played a role in Turner's concentration, in the first decade of his career, on castles, ruined abbeys, and Gothic cathedrals, since such images were popular and marketable. Yet in his sketches of these subjects Turner displays an inquisitive interest that seems to transcend cold economic calculation. In 1791, for instance, he devoted much of a sketchbook to views of Malmsbury Abbey from virtually every angle.

Turner's finished watercolors were made from composites of such sketches; they were accurate while, according to Cosmo Monkhouse, "supressing those facts which jarred his scheme of form and color."[4] This tendency led Ruskin, who rarely expressed a negative sentiment toward Turner, to conclude: "Turner never got thoroughly into the feeling of Gothic, its darkness and complexity embarrased him; he was apt to whiten by way of idealizing it and to cast aside its details in order to get breadth of delicate light."[5]

Even Turner's earliest drawings of ruins represent what his biographer Walter Thornbury called scenes

not as they were, but as they are — contrasting feudal and the past as much as possible, and as sadly as possible, with the present... There is one thing Turner will always show us in a ruined castle, and that is, that it is a work of a far receding and contrasting age.[6]

In the years around the turn of the century, Turner changed from a topographical draftsman into a painter of the wider world of landscape, abandoning his safe and comfortable employment as a leading provider of Gothic images to periodicals and the public. Henceforth Turner divided his attention between watercolor and oil painting. He did not give up the depiction of ruins; instead, the ruins merely became what they truthfully were—occurences in the landscape.

Turner revealed his break with the past in a sketchbook he carried with him on a visit to Scotland in the summer of 1801. In his *Scottish Landscape with Castle and Bridge*, for instance, the landscape predominates (fig. 41). The castle,

42
Watercolor on white paper:
Borthwick Castle. *J.M.W. Turner, 1818.*
Gift of Mr. and Mrs Kurt F. Pantzer, Sr.
72.70.9, Indianapolis Museum of Art

presumably Linlithgow, assumes no greater importance than the trees before it. The bridge and figures are probably figments of Turner's imagination. That the castle is not clearly identifiable is significant in view of Turner's previous employment as an illustrator of topographical sites.

Seventeen years later Turner again concentrated his brush on Gothic architecture. He was employed as one of the artists whose work appeared in *Provincial Antiquities and Picturesque Scenery of Scotland* (1818-1826), to which the great Scottish writer Sir Walter Scott contributed essays on Scotland's most important monuments. Scott reportedly wished to employ only Scottish artists on the project, but the publishers insisted on engaging the renowned Turner. In 1818, Turner journeyed north to make preparatory sketches for the ten watercolors that would appear, in the form of engravings, in *Provincial Antiquities.*

43
Watercolor on white paper:
Roslin Castle, Hawthornden.
J.M.W. Turner, ca. 1820.
Gift of Mr. and Mrs Kurt F. Pantzer, Sr.
72.70.10, Indianapolis Museum of Art

Works from this series, such as *Borthwick Castle* (fig. 42) and *Roslin Castle, Hawthornden* (fig. 43), reemphasize Turner's association of architecture with nature. In each case the elements — air, water, earth — and man play a decisive role in Turner's presentation of the castle as an ancient, almost forgotten, still awe-inspiring remnant of the past.

Such an approach is remarkably, though unconsciously, compatible with the spirit of Scott's corresponding essays. Scott, like Turner, used each monument as a point of departure to a wider world. In his essays, Scott quickly dispenses with physical descriptions and moves on to the retelling of the old legends, histories, and the remembrances he associates with the sites. Massive Borthwick and haunted Roslin echoed with stories of the past, which had stirred the author's imagination from boyhood.

In 1831, Turner was asked to direct his talents once again to Gothic architecture, and Scott was again his collaborator. Heeding the recommendation of his publisher, Robert Cadell, Scott invited Turner to illustrate his *Poetical Works*. Turner traveled to Scotland in August 1831 to sketch the castles, abbeys, and landscapes that were appropriate to the text and significant in the author's life. The sites were chosen by Scott and Cadell, but the interpretations were Turner's. Following the tendency of Turner's recent work, these castled landscapes are more broadly brushed and less detailed than his contributions to the *Provincial Antiquities*. In a watercolor such as *Smailholm Tower* (fig. 44), the distant past and Scott's past

44
Watercolor on white paper:
Smailholm Tower. *J.M.W. Turner, ca. 1831.*
Gift in memory of
Dr. and Mrs. Hugo O. Pantzer
by their children

45
Oil on canvas: The Departure.
Thomas Cole, 1837.
Gift of William Wilson Corcoran,
In the collection of the
Corcoran Gallery of Art,
Washington, D.C.

are neatly mingled. Smailholm Tower, which stood on the property of Scott's grandfather, was the ruin that first stirred the author's youthful imagination to thoughts of knightly dash and glory.

Turner and Scott visualized a ruin as a natural place —as much a part of their world as of the past. Minute detail and architectural accuracy were subordinated to the wider harmony of nature and the broader vistas of their creative imaginations. Their attitude toward the Gothic period was typical of the early nineteenth century. From the early days of the Gothic Revival, the ruined shell of a castle or abbey had been more an object of artistic reverie than of antiquarian reverence — a fact recognized by John Ruskin. In his opinion, Turner and Scott best exemplified the devotion to landscape and medievalism that marked their time; he therefore singled out these two artists as "the greatest representatives of the mind and age in painting and literature."[7]

Ellwood C. Parry III

Towers Above the Trees in Romantic Landscape Paintings

In May 1835, the popular American landscape painter, Thomas Cole (1801-1848), contrasted European and American scenery in a lecture to the American Lyceum in New York. In one significant portion of his address, Cole lamented the inevitable fact that the scenery of the New World, no matter how beautiful or sublime, always lacked historical associations tied to architectural remains from earlier ages. While arguing that the United States, as a new nation, was not completely devoid of legendary and historical sites of interest, he had to admit that American associations were not so much of the past as of the present and the future.

The Rhine has its castled crags, its vine-clad hills and ancient villages; the Hudson has its wooded mountains, its rugged precipices, its green undulating shores — a natural majesty, and an unbounded capacity for improvement by art. Its shores are not yet besprinkled with venerated ruins, or the palaces of princes; but there are flourishing towns, and neat villas, and the hand of taste has already been at work. Without any great stretch of the imagination we may anticipate the time when the ample waters shall reflect temple, and tower, and dome, in every variety of picturesqueness and magnificence.[1]

Since Greco-Roman temples, Gothic towers, and golden pleasure domes abound in Cole's imaginative pictures of the 1830s and 1840s, his art and ideas offer a perfect vantage point from which to glimpse the towers above the trees in both British and American landscape paintings of the Romantic era.

Cole was born and raised in Lancashire near the English Lake District; he emigrated with his family to North America in 1818. Coming from such a background, he was undoubtedly aware of the time–lag involved when new aesthetic ideals, emanating from London, crossed the ocean successfully. As he openly admitted in his discussion of American scenery, there was never a question of the survival of medieval castles or cathedrals to influence later generations on this side of the Atlantic.

In the first decades of the new republic, portraiture remained the dominant category of American picture-making, just as it had throughout Colonial times. Any hints of a taste for Gothic imagery are extremely hard to

46
Oil on canvas:
The Bard.
John Martin, 1817.
Yale Center
for British Art,
Paul Mellon
Collection

find amid the myriad portraits and occasional figure paintings of the Federal period. And at the start of the nineteenth century, the situation was not much different in terms of landscape painting in the United States: next to nothing of a Gothic nature appeared.

A handful of British landscape painters and printmakers had arrived during the 1790s, but none of them was skilled or as adventurous as Thomas Girtin or J.M.W. Turner, whose watercolors were rapidly advancing in technique and subject matter from topographical renderings of picturesque palaces and ruined priories to sweeping vistas of Tintern Abbey or Norham Castle, done with breathtaking light effects. In 1808–1809, when William Birch, a miniaturist and enamel painter trained in England, published a series of twenty hand-colored plates entitled *Country Seats of the United States*, only one depicted a rural residence in the Gothic style. That was Sedgeley, outside of Philadelphia, designed by Benjamin Latrobe and built in 1799, a modest two-story house with pointed-arch window openings and graceful trees dotting its lawns.

It was not until after the war of 1812 that American architects — who were followed in time by a new generation of Romantic landscape painters that included Cole — began to catch up with their counterparts in the British Isles. Previous attempts to introduce the manner of the Middle Ages for domestic or ecclesiastical buildings had resulted in the construction of only a few isolated examples. But the dramatic appearance of Trinity Church on the Green in New Haven, designed and built from 1814 to 1817 by Ithiel Town, marked the beginning of a new era in which many practitioners, besides Latrobe, made concerted efforts to import a more authentic medieval style to the United States. A wave of publications on medieval architecture, originating in London after the end of the Napoleonic wars, fostered and promoted the surge of popular and professional interest in the Gothic.

A few wealthy Americans demonstrated their enthusiasm for the Gothic style when building their own homes. Daniel Wadsworth, for example, built an impressive country residence in the picturesque Gothic style sometime before 1820. Called Monte Video, this estate occupied an elevated ledge on the west side of Talcott Mountain, near Hartford, Connecticut. If Wadsworth might easily have imagined himself as a feudal lord, master of all he surveyed from his mountain retreat, Robert Gilmor, Jr., took even greater pains to make sure

47
Oil on panel:
Mediterranean Coast
Scene with Tower,
Thomas Cole, after 1832.
Albany Institute of
History and Art

48
Oil on canvas:
Hadleigh Castle,
John Constable, 1829.
Yale Center for
British Art,
Paul Mellon Collection

49
*Colored wood engraving
after a design by John Constable:*
Yonder Ivy-Mantled Tower,
*from "Elegy Written
in a Country Church-Yard,"
by Thomas Gray, 1836.
Yale Center for British
Art, Paul Mellon Collection*

that his new home, Glen Ellen, was as castle-like as possible. Inspired by Abbotsford, the home of Sir Walter Scott, Gilmor, in 1832, commissioned the architectural firm of Ithiel Town and Alexander Jackson Davis to design a striking asymmetrical Gothic manor house to grace the estate he and a brother had purchased along the Gunpowder River north of Baltimore.

Scott's historical novels of the 1820s were enormously popular in the United States, and this popularity helped to promote the quickening interest in Gothic residences as well as churches, all marked by increasingly authentic details. In American architectural circles, the firm of Town and Davis was unquestionably the major beneficiary of the gradual shift away from the rational forms of the Greek Revival. Davis, in particular, had a special talent for Gothic detail. He designed a number of Gothic residences for well-to-do patrons during the late 1830s, with the result that Gothic towers, turrets, pinnacles, and crenellated cornice lines sprang up in wood and stone along the banks of the Hudson, just as Thomas Cole had predicted they would.

Looking back, it seems far from accidental that the spread of the Gothic Revival in America, a trend that clearly began to accelerate in the 1820s and 1830s, coincided with the emergence of an American trend in Romantic landscape painting, namely, the Hudson River School. Indeed, Wadsworth and Gilmor were important patrons of the young Cole. They began to buy his work not long after he had moved to New York in 1825, a date that marks the real beginning of his professional career as a painter. Their willingness to acquire not only Cole's topographical scenes of the remote mountain areas of New England and upstate New York, but also examples of his more ambitious imaginative pictures, seems symbolic of America's apparently unquenchable thirst for the Romantic, whether in nature, art, or architecture.

More than any other member of the first generation of the Hudson River School, Cole strove for sublime effects which he knew would please his audience. During the first phase of his mature career (1825–1829), Cole used every technique as a landscape painter — storm-blasted trees, dangerous precipices, plunging cataracts, mysterious rocking stones, and even an erupting volcano — to make scenes from the Bible or James Fenimore Cooper's *Last of the Mohicans* (1826) appear even wilder, more exalted, or more terrifying.

By dwarfing his foreground figures, who often seem about to be engulfed by the power and vastness of nature, Cole followed a pattern already established in England by Turner and by the slightly younger John Martin. Turner's and Martin's historical landscapes of the 1810s and 1820s were often set in ancient Egypt or Babylon, classical Carthage, or even medieval Wales. Although these artists made use of buildings in their epic narrative scenes, architectural backdrops did not play a significant role in Cole's work until after his three-year stay in Europe.

Cole arrived in London in the summer of 1829, in time to see several impressive landscapes by Turner and John Constable at the Royal Academy exhibition. While in England, Cole visited Turner's studio and recorded his impressions of the man and his art. He probably met Martin, although the evidence for this is conjectural, and he was certainly accepted into the circle of artists around Constable and his American friend, Charles Robert Leslie.

Discussions about methods of introducing appropriate architectural elements into landscape must have come up frequently among these painters. And Cole must have absorbed a great deal of information both from the artists he met and from their pictures and publications. It is certainly clear that after his stay in London, this American artist was commited to the pictorial value of having real or imaginary buildings in all of his historical landscape paintings as a theme-enhancing backdrop, rich in associations.

Evidence of English influence is not hard to find in Cole's imaginative works after his return from Europe in 1832. The Greco-Roman civilization so eloquently evoked by Turner in several pictures of the rise and fall of Carthage, found a convincing echo in Cole's more carefully orchestrated series of five paintings, *The Course of Empire*, commissioned from 1833 to 1836. Into these works Cole poured all sorts of learned allusions to the art and architecture of the ancient Mediterranean world.

After this decidedly neoclassical series, Gothic structures began to appear in Cole's art in increasing numbers. In 1837, for instance, Cole completed a pair of large landscape compositions, *The Departure* (fig. 45) and *The Return*, which he called "Scenes Illustrative of Feudal Manners and Times." In *The Departure*, Cole deliberately tried to graft his picture onto the same tradition as Martin's illustrations for Thomas Gray's epic poem *The Bard* (fig. 46). Admittedly, Cole softened the jagged

50
Oil on cardboard: Study for Past.
Thomas Cole, 1838.
Amherst College,
Mead Art Museum

51
Oil on cardboard: Study for Present.
Thomas Cole, 1838.
Amherst College,
Mead Art Museum

52
Oil on canvas:
Sunset Through a Ruined Abbey.
Francis Danby, ca. 1825–30.
Courtesy of the
Tate Gallery, London

landscape, brought the castle down to a lower elevation, and turned the bard's curse into a pilgrim's farewell, but the configuration of a knight and his soldiers riding out from their stronghold remains essentially the same.

In the companion picture, *The Return*, Cole portrayed the same knight being carried back from the war on a litter. This somber tableau seems to summarize the imagery of Thomas Gray's *Elegy written in a Country Church-yard*, which had just been reissued in London with illustrations by Constable. All in all, so many round but riven towers looming up in melancholy solitude in Cole's landscapes of the 1830s, such as the *Mediterranean Coast Scene with Tower* (fig. 47), suggest the strong influence of Constable's *Hadleigh Castle* (fig. 48) or even of his more poetic *Ivy-Mantled Tower* (fig. 49).

After seeing *The Departure* and *The Return*, a wealthy collector commissioned Cole, in 1838, to paint a similar pair of landscapes in the Gothic mode. The compositional

53
Oil on canvas: Hawking Party
in the Time of Queen Elizabeth.
Jasper Francis Cropsey, 1853.
Courtesy of the
Newington-Cropsey Foundation

sketches and final versions of *Past* and *Present* (figs. 50 and 51) represent another variation on the before–and–after theme that so delighted Romantic artists both here and abroad. Cleverly borrowing from image traditions that can be traced back at least as far as Peter Paul Rubens' *Tournament before the Château de Steen* (circa 1635–1640), Cole was able to stage a convincing jousting match in the foreground of *Past*, thereby giving his viewer a delicious taste of "the boast of heraldry [and] the pomp of power."[2]

Cole had more freedom than practicing architects A.J. Davis or Andrew Jackson Downing, who had to make their Gothic castles, villas, and cottages habitable for growing families of the late 1830s. He could fill pages of his sketchbooks with design after design until he found exactly the right asymmetrical silhouette for the castles that dominate the middle ground in both *The Departure* (fig. 45) and *Past* (fig. 50).

As a builder in paint, Cole could also have the story-telling fun of destroying what he had just erected on such a grand scale. In his *Present* (fig. 51) Cole kept the massive round tower or keep of the castle in virtually the same position, relative to the viewer's eye, that it occupied in *Past*. But this time, as if through the trick of time-lapse photography, eons have passed. What was once a proud and glorious monument to human ambition is now a pitiful overgrown skeleton. In front of this reminder of the rotation of the wheel of fortune, a solitary shepherd with a staff contemplates the setting sun — just as a similar figure, holding a spear, watches the last slanting rays of light in Francis Danby's *Sunset through a Ruined Abbey* (fig. 52). Whether Cole had met Danby or seen his work in London is questionable. What is significant is that both men seem to share a fascination with back-lighting effects.

Cole seems to have been more interested in depicting Gothic buildings than any other American landscape painter. When younger men such as John Frederick Kensett (1816–1872) and Sanford Robinson Gifford (1823–1880) went to Europe in the 1840s and 1850s, they sketched famous castles in much the same way that Cole had done on earlier journeys. When his close friend, Asher B. Durand (1796–1886), turned to landscape painting in 1840, it was Cole's example that inspired the Greek and Gothic buildings in his works. And when Cole died unexpectedly in 1848, Durand painted an indirect tribute to his friend in *Landscape: Scene from 'Thanatopsis'* (1850) which contains an imaginary castle on a promontory in the distance, and a funeral ceremony under the ancient oak trees not far from a Gothic church in the middle ground.

As late as the 1850s, when Jasper F. Cropsey (1823–1900) painted *Queen Elizabeth's Hawking Party* and *The Spirit of War* (figs. 53 and 54), he too was paying homage to Cole as an inspired director of costume epics set in the Middle Ages. After the mid-1850s, however, American interest shifted radically. Instead of actual or imagined Gothic towers above the trees, it was the Rocky Mountains or the Sierra Nevada, the icebergs of the North, and even the active volcanos of South America that delighted the public. In the years just before and after the Civil War, westward expansion and the promise of a glorious future eclipsed, at least for a time, any lingering fascination with the medieval past.

54
Oil on canvas:
The Spirit of War.
Jasper Francis Cropsey, 1851.
Courtesy of the
National Gallery of Art,
Washington, D.C.,
Avalon Fund

Naomi Reed Kline *The Popular Explosion*

y the second half of the nineteenth century the taste for the medieval had become so prevalent that it provided the impetus for a veritable explosion of modern castle building and castle imagery. The disdain for the medieval that marked the dominant Classicism of the eighteenth century — a disdain only partially challenged by the Gothic Revival — was finally dissipated in the nineteenth century. Authoritative volumes of medieval history appeared throughout Europe, dividing the thousand years previously considered as a single era into discrete periods and artistic styles. Saxons were distinguished from Goths, Romanesque art and architecture from Gothic.

From the vantage point of the nineteenth century, the Middle Ages began to be viewed romantically as a simpler, more ordered time, free from the social turbulence and chaos of the Industrial Revolution. Scott's works had woven history and fiction together, giving flesh and blood to the Middle Ages. Thomas Carlyle, the Victorian philosopher and historian, provided an intellectual climate for medieval nostalgia in his little book, Past and Present, published in 1843.

Enthusiasm for the medieval had spread well beyond England. By the turn of the century the Gothic Revival had reached France, where the first museum dedicated solely to medieval artifacts was established. This collection, in turn, produced a spate of creative interest in medieval art and architecture. The German brand of Romanticism incorporated medieval subject matter, producing art and literature tinged with the concept of the sublime. Thus, alongside the growing compendia of facts unearthed about the Middle Ages, new fictions continued to be created, especially in the realm of architecture, where real castles inspired new versions.

Eugène Viollet-le-Duc, the French architect and scholar of medieval architecture, published his exhaustive, ten volume Dictionnaire raisonné de l'architecture française du XI⁰ au XVI⁰ siècle *(1854–1869) and was commissioned to restore numerous medieval buildings. His restoration of the fortifications at Carcassone (1852–1879) (fig. 55) and his reconstruction of the castle of Pierrefonds (1859–1870) for Louis Napoleon, although based on sound architectural scholarship, added a plethora of crenellations and turrets, which imparted a fairy tale quality to the architecture. Inspired by the work at Pierrefonds, King*

55
Carcasonne, Town and Citadel.
Restored by Viollet-le-Duc, 1852–79.
Photograph: Richard Cassady

Ludwig II of Bavaria (1848–1886), known as "Mad Ludwig," took Viollet's concepts to their extreme and built Neuschwanstein (fig. 56), a structure which is said to have influenced Disney's imaginative castles.

Set against these princely pretensions were the yearnings of a new class of industrial magnates who sought to legitimize their meteoric rise to wealth with the accoutrements of royalty. They used the revitalized architectural symbol of the castle to try to dominate the cultural, and physical, landscape of their age. By the turn of the twentieth century a rash of modern castles had been built. It is striking that the phenomenon gained enormous impetus in the "classless" society of America. James F. O'Gorman's essay, Castle Building in America, *offers insights into this ironic phenomenon of castle–building on American soil.*

The technological developments of the nineteenth century allowed people and information to travel at a pace previously unknown. Books and ideas crossed the Atlantic at furious speed. Travelers replaced their sketchbooks with cameras. Picture postcards, stereoscope views, and travel guides were placed on shelves beside books and family photo albums (fig. 57). A growing number of illustrated fictional romances became available. Decorative objects, often with medieval themes such as souvenir ceramics and sets of china, were mass–produced (fig. 58). Images of European castles were firmly ensconced in American homes, helping to keep the fantasy of castles alive in the popular imagination.

Scott's novels had paved the way for Tennyson's poetic adaptions of Arthurian legends, and for new currents in the visual arts. The famous Moxon edition of Tennyson's Poems, *published in 1847, was illustrated not with the picturesque castles that appeared in editions of Scott, but with figural illustrations of haunting beauty (fig. 59) by William Holman Hunt (1827–1910), Dante Gabriel Rossetti (1828–1882), and John Everett Millais (1829–1896), all founding members of the pre-Raphaelite Brotherhood.*

In the midst of the Victorian age and the Industrial Revolution, the pre-Raphaelites rejected the ideals of the conservative Royal Academy. They chose, rather, to work in the tradition of medieval artists or, more precisely, in artistic traditions that pre-dated the Renaissance tenets of Raphael, still considered the exemplar of artistic virtue in most respected quarters. William Morris (1834–1896), another member of the pre-Raphaelite Brotherhood, helped found the Arts and Crafts movement, which fostered craftsmanship in a period of machine technology.

56
Neuschwanstein, Bavaria.
Photograph courtesy of
the German Information Center

57
*Windsor Castle
from the Meadows.
Valentine photograph
courtesy of
Stephen T. Rose
Gallery*

Perhaps the most sustained current of this burgeoning of medieval imagery in art, literature, and architecture was within the realm of children's books, discussed by Patricia Dooley in her essay, The Castle in Children's Storybooks. *Through the world of fairy tales and fantasy, children were exposed to the bygone medieval era of castles and a fabricated mythology of kings and queens, and knights in shining armor. Enjoying a prosperity that was in part financed by the factory labor of working-class children, the Victorian middle class created a cult of the family and childhood. Books geared to the fantasies of childhood proliferated. Modern translations and illustrated versions of Charles Perrault's* Histoires ou contes du temps passé avec des moralités *(1697) and Jacob and Wilhelm Grimm's* Kinder- und Hausmärchen *(1812-1815) — to mention only two — were joined by Sir Walter Scott's* Tales of a Grandfather *(1827), the works of Hans Christian Andersen (1805–1875), and the genre of the art fairy tale.*

Who can venture to say how many real-life castle-builders were in truth acting out their childhood fantasies of castles, creating an architectural symbol of all the romantic baggage they had accumulated in their lifetimes? Ludwig of Bavaria, for instance, the builder of Neuschwanstein, had been infatuated since his boyhood with the works of Richard Wagner and with the medieval heroics of German legend so often translated into opera (fig. 60). As a child he had often stayed at Schloss Hohenschwangau, which his father, Maximilian II, had restored as a neo-Gothic fortress and which Moritz von Schwind had decorated with murals illustrating the story of the swan-knight Lohengrin.

By the turn of the century, castles and knights, princes and princesses, had become a universal fantasy. In America a school of illustrators, fascinated by these themes, emerged to work on the immense number of books and periodicals for young and

58
*English Majolica Castles,
ca. 1830–40.
Society for
the Preservation of
New England Antiquities.
Photograph:
J. David Bohl*

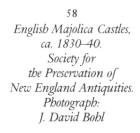

59
Engraving: The Palace of Art,
by Dante Gabriel Rosetti, 1857,
from Tennyson's Poems.
Courtesy of the Houghton Library,
Harvard University

old that romantically revived the Middle Ages.

Edwin Austin Abbey (1852–1911) illustrated Shakespearean stories in the pre-Raphaelite style for the readers of Scribner's and Harper's Weekly. He also meticulously researched and painted a monumental mural of the story of the Holy Grail for the delivery room of the Boston Public Library. Abbey chose to live most of his life in England, where he was in touch with the countryside that inspired Shakespeare and the pre-Raphaelites. He was succeeded by illustrators who were influenced by his style, but who used the landscape and traditions of America as their major source of inspiration.

The American tradition of illustration dispensed with the quasi-religious overtones of the pre-Raphaelites and was concerned more with fanciful works of a decorative nature. Howard Pyle, an innovator in the field, showed the way for a veritable league of artists. As an author-illustrator, Pyle was sensitive to the relationship of word and picture. His reworkings of Arthurian legends, his Merry Adventures of Robin Hood *(1883), and* Otto of the Silver Hand *(1888) brought the pre-Raphaelites' stylization of medieval subject matter to popular American culture. His work was to prove the inspiration for such distinguished illustrators as N.C. Wyeth (1882–1945) and Maxfield Parrish (1870–1966). The works of these illustrators are discussed in Elizabeth Hawkes' essay,* Of Knights and Castles: Illustrations by Howard Pyle and His Students.

American illustrators made little distinction between childhood and adulthood when they directed their work to an audience. Their illustrations had a simplicity and directness that appealed simultaneously to young and old. Thus there was little to separate Parrish's fantasies on Scribner's *covers from those on the front of* St. Nicholas, *the most successful and literate of American children's magazines of the time. His magical illustrations used the element of childhood fantasy to appeal to a universal audience (fig. 61).*

The world of children's literature is clearly central to any discussion of the role of the castle in the popular imagination. But perhaps the most telling example of the imaginative strength the castle has acquired in the popular mind lies, not in the work of the professional artist, but in the symbolic vocabulary of our dreams. Centuries after their practical purpose has vanished, castles continue to be present, whether they are of stone or mortar, or creations of our imagination. Havens of security, symbols of power and wealth, or vessels for our fantasies, these ancient fortresses continue to populate the landscapes of our lives.

60
Engraving from color aquatint by
Karl Friedrich Schinkel, 1820:
"Burg Ringstaedten."
Set for the last scene of the
opera Undine *by Lortzing.*
Courtesy of the Cooper-Hewitt Museum,
The Smithsonian Institution's
National Museum of Design

61
Oil on paper: Air Castles.
Maxfield Parrish.
Private Collection,
Courtesy of La Galeria,
San Mateo, California.
Photograph: Fred English

James F. O'Gorman *Castle Building in America, or What Scott Hath Wrought*

In *Life on the Mississippi* (1883) Mark Twain paused at Baton Rouge to reflect upon the cultural origins of the Louisiana State capitol, erected between 1847 and 1850 from the design of James Dakin:

Sir Walter Scott is probably responsible for the Capitol building; for it is not conceivable that this little sham castle would ever have been built if he had not run the people mad, a couple of generations ago, with his medieval romances... By itself the imitation castle is doubtless harmless... but as a symbol and breeder and sustainer of maudlin Middle-Age romanticism here in the midst of the plainest and sturdiest and infinitely greatest and worthiest of all centuries the world has seen, it is necessarily a hurtful thing and a mistake.

Twain spotted the inherent contradiction represented by architecture, of the period after the Industrial Revolution, wrapped in medieval period costume. He also perceived its cause in literary association. A century nursed on the castle-dotted tales of "merry old England" in Scott's Waverly novels (the first, *Waverly*, was published in 1814) found it appropriate to dress buildings in suggestive forms. The influence of these historical romances was magnified in mid-nineteenth-century America through novels and popular periodicals, such as *Gleason's* and *Ballou's*, in which frequent views of medieval piles such as Windsor or Warwick vied for the reader's attention with fanciful full-page illustrations of the storming of old English castles. The resulting wave of American castle-building was not restricted to public architecture, nor did it die with good Queen Victoria.

By the nineteenth century a vast inventory of styles could be applied by architects to the wide range of building types ordered by an increasingly pluralistic society. Roman classicism served for banks and engineering works; Greek classicism seemed appropriate for governmental and urban buildings; exotic Eastern forms served for light-hearted recreational usage as well as synagogue design; and a medieval vocabulary, especially Gothic or pointed details, evoked the supposed piety of the Middle Ages in churches of a variety of denominations.

Among revived medieval modes was the castellated. To some nineteenth- and twentieth-century eyes, this seemed to constitute suitable dress for buildings where, at least, the semblance of a fortified outer shell was desired. Such buildings included jails, armories, academies (whether military or otherwise), convents, some government buildings, and some hotels. In addition, railroad stations,

62

Engraving: Eastern State Penitentiary of Pennsylvania by C. G. Childs, 1829, after drawing by William Mason. Courtesy of the Historical Society of Pennsylvania

residences, and a host of other types might occasionally sport a fittingly battlemented silhouette.

John Haviland's Eastern State Penitentiary in Philadelphia, erected between 1823 and 1829 and presenting to the world a fortified gateway complete with portcullis, established the castellated profile for prison architecture (fig. 62). Twain quotes the description of a "Female Academy" in Tennessee which resembled "the old castles of song and story, with its towers, turreted walls, and ivy-mantled porches." Military schools customarily borrowed medieval forms, following such leads as the granite "New Barracks" erected at West Point in the 1850s. The developing railroad station frequently found appropriate shape in the castellated silhouette. This was justified by analogy: the station was a gateway to the city, and the medieval civic portal was typically fortified. Castellated hotels appealed to the public, perhaps because a holiday is "unreal" time, and so appropriately spent in a fantasy world. The same concept shapes today's hostelries (such as the Sheraton-Tara in Massachusetts) where "buxom wenches" serve ale in "pubs" at the base of a battle-mented tower which sprouts paste-on bartizans.

Armories and arsenals cry out for battlemented treatment, and function joined symbol in a number of those erected after the Civil War. Burnham and Root's First Regiment Armory in Chicago (1889-1891), built in the era of the Haymarket Riots, expressed its purpose as a defensive bastion in the time of civil strife with seventy-five-foot-high solid stone walls, an iron portcullis, machicolated parapet, and bartizans from which defenders could rake the outside walls (fig. 63). No sham castle this!

These and other structures represent the variety of types of castle-building in America, but the castellated structure which has captured popular imagination is the residence. Since common usage and some writers apply the term "castle" indiscriminately to houses either imposing because of age or size, one must begin with a definition — and what better definition than one which springs from Scott's era, the heart of the Romantic movement?

The horticulturist Andrew Jackson Downing (1815-1852), an arbiter of taste in nineteenth-century America, adapted to the New World the picturesque movement which originated in England in the eighteenth century. In seminal works such as *The Theory and Practice of Landscape Gardening* (1841), Downing offered a variety of revived styles suitable to the reshaping of American domestic architecture.

Among these modes was the castellated. According to Downing such a residence above all wanted "battlements cut out of the solid parapet . . . generally conceal[ing] the roof." The exterior should display "strong and massive octagonal or circular towers," and pointed, square, or mixed windows should open the walls. In the main, wrote Downing, modern castles "preserve the general character of the ancient castle, while they combine with it almost every modern luxury." Although Downing anticipated Twain's concern about the fitness of the castellated residence for industrial America, finding it "too ambitious and expensive . . . for a republic, where landed estates are not secured by entail," he nonetheless believed "there is no weighty reason why a wealthy proprietor should not erect his mansion in the castellated style, if that style is in unison with his scenery and locality."

Downing well understood the taste of his audience, and he knew the castellated mode would fulfill their popular Scottish dreams:

63
First Regiment Armory, Chicago. Burnham and Root, Architects, 1889–91. Photograph courtesy of the Art Institute of Chicago

RESIDENCE OF S. L. CARLETON, PORTLAND, MAINE.

64
Residence of S.L. Carleton,
Portland, Maine, ca. 1854.
Photograph: Earle G. Shettleworth, Jr.

The literature of Europe . . . is so much our own, that we form a kind of delightful acquaintance with the venerable castles, abbeys, and strongholds of the middle ages . . . A castellated residence . . . in a wild and picturesque situation, may be interesting not only from its being perfectly in keeping with surrounding nature, but from the delightful manner in which it awakens associations fraught with the most enticing history of the past.[1]

Downing clearly saw the castellated residence in America as the embodiment of the views published in such current popular English picture books as *Landscape Illustrations of the Waverly Novels* (1832), in which nearly every page presents another castellated rustic scene immortalized by Scott. And he clearly understood the castle as the paradigm of the picturesque: an irregular silhouette in a jagged setting.

The history of American domestic castle-building stretches from Downing's day well into the twentieth century. Not all precedents were English, and probably not all castle-builders read Scott, nor all castle architects Downing. Still, the romantic picturesque pervades the entire movement. So, too, there is a common denominator or collective profile to be found among those who ordered castellated homes.

These patrons were, of course, possessed of some degree of wealth, even if they were not all in a league with William Randolph Hearst. Most were industrious, many inventive. They were largely self-made men whose castles manifested to themselves and the world that they had arrived at positions where long-deferred dreams might finally be fulfilled. Some were reclusive, but others were extroverts, accustomed to the public eye. One group had childhood memories of European castles; another, memories of historic sites visited in the Old World; and a third, as vivid an image from a popular novel or magazine. Some sought to emulate in literature the writings of their favorite authors. Many cultivated a taste for other arts, including music. They were as a rule uncommonly intelligent. Few were what they seemed to the populace beyond the portcullis. They were unusual men, yes, but not unfettered. And collectively they fulfilled, whatever their individual motivations, the castellated mission of the romantic picturesque.

Early castellated residences reflect the influence of Scott and Downing. A visit to Scott's own battlemented home, Abbotsford, often led to transformations in the homes of

Americans, sometimes with unforeseen results. James Fenimore Cooper returned from Europe to nail wooden battlements above the eaves of his Federal house at Cooperstown, New York, thus stopping the roof drainage and inundating the interior. *Gleason's* in 1854 wrote of the castellated residence of daguerreotypist Samuel L. Carleton in Portland, Maine (fig. 64), that "no person of letters or taste can look on the outside without a rush of shades flitting before him . . . of the days of ancient chivalry and knight errantry, and memories chanting . . . [Scott's] 'lay of the last minstrel.' " The Hudson River became the Rhine of the New World, with simulated castles such as Edwin Forrest's Fonthill (named after Beckford's Fonthill Abbey) lining its banks in suitably picturesque array.

With the aftermath of the Civil War came changes, but not in the potency of Scott's influence. Hundred Oaks in

65
Grey Towers, Glenside, Pennsylvania.
Horace Trumbauer,
Architect, 1893–98.
Photograph courtesy of
Beaver College

Winchester, Tennessee, by 1892 had assumed a rich collection of castellated brick forms ready to receive a soothing mantle of ivy transplanted from Abbotsford. Within, the library was a copy of Scott's.

The period after the Civil War was characterized by the growth of the nation in wealth and ambition, and this in turn was reflected in the increased cost and dimensions of castellated homes. By previous American standards Grey Towers (now Beaver College) in Glenside, Pennsylvania, a work of the 1880s by Horace Trumbauer, is huge (fig. 65). More importantly, it was intended to recall Alnwick Castle in Northumberland. The use of a specific Old World source as a model, accurate or not, while it can be found in some mid-century examples, became more common as the century advanced and scholarship in architectural history developed more precise information about prototypes. The vaguely suggestive battlemented silhouette

66

*The first White Castle: concrete block construction.
Opened in March, 1929,
in Wichita, Kansas. A contemporary
photograph.*

67

White Castle: white enamel glazed brick. Opened in July, 1930, on upper Broadway in New York City.

68

White Castle: white textured porcelain enamel. Opened in September, 1932, on Hempstead Turnpike, New York.

69

White Castle: white porcelain enamel, steel sheets on a steel frame. Opened in May, 1973, in St. Louis.

70
Hammond Castle Museum,
Gloucester, Massachusetts.
Allen and Collens,
Architects, 1926–29.
Photograph:
Jean Baer O'Gorman

of Downing's day no longer sufficed for some builders.
Precise re-creation, or at least the intention to be precise,
whether obtained by new design or acquisition of antique
fragments in Europe, was frequently the order of this day.
Archaeology reformed romance in these late nineteenth-
and early twentieth-century abodes.

By the twentieth century what Twain and Downing
considered the inappropriateness of the castle in America
seemed even more pronounced, as the picturesque gave
way to mechanized methods, new materials, and the need
for economy in construction. Such is the elasticity of the
human imagination, however, that while an international-
style castle seems at first to boggle the mind, the buildings
of the White Castle (figs. 66-69) fast-food chain achieved
just that dichotomous synthesis. In any event, castle-
building had always seemed an extraordinary activity, and
it now became positively eccentric.

Scott's influence proved tenacious, surviving the age of
factories to influence the age of jazz. The Waverly novels
marched upright across the shelves of the library of John

Hays Hammond, Jr. who, with the help of architect Harold Willis, erected his eclectic castle on the western shore of Gloucester harbor in the 1920s (fig.70).

What Twain ungraciously called Scott's "windy humbuggeries" seem to blow through the rhetoric of the builder of another American castle: "Chateau Laroche was built as an expression and reminder of the simple strength and rugged grandeur of the mighty men who lived when Knighthood was in flower."

As is indeed the case. The quotation is found in a booklet published in 1980 by Harry D. Andrews the builder (from 1929 on) of Chatcau Laroche in Loveland, Ohio and the self-styled "Seneschal" of the Knights of the Golden Trail headquartered therein. As Twain remarked, aptly, "the man that can blow so complacent a blast . . . probably blows it from a castle."

Although the fanciful and the theatrical shaped many twentieth-century castles, the urge to re-create European settings — to transport to America medieval buildings and attendant associations — grew more intense. As late as 1930, William Randolph Hearst employed Julia Morgan to re-create Wyntoon Castle from the fragments of the Spanish convent of Santa Maria de Oliva, which he had shipped from abroad. The drawings for this unrealized dream show a multi-towercd citadel with provisions for a fan-vaulted bowling alley and a swimming pool occupying the nave, transepts, and apse of a church. Even Downing had said that a new castle might preserve the general character of an old one, while it incorporated "almost every modern luxury."

It might be expected that castles would disappear for economic reasons, during and after the Depression, or that the appeal of Scott would diminish. It would be unwise to assume so. A stone castellated residence which cannot be ten years old rides the crest of a hill near the coast at Malibu Beach, California, and Philip Johnson recently designed a castellated brick skyscraper for lower Manhattan (fig. 71).

But it is true that castle-building went democratic when it reached the popular level, during the Depression and after, in the White Castles, the fantasy worlds of Disney, or the slumberlands of the castellated hotels. While these may be of questionable architectural quality, they represent in their own debased forms a lingering, if waning, association with Scott's medieval romances.

Patricia Dooley *The Castle in Children's Storybooks*

Castles have a unique hold on the popular imagination. In our culture, no other kind of building commands such wide recognition and such sentimental allegiance. One sign of the importance of the castle is its place in the illustrated children's book — the source of much popular imagery. Only the lowly cottage, among all other building types, appears so frequently in storybooks for children.

Books designed specifically for children began to appear in the 1740s in England; they drew for their imagery on a long history of popular and luxury illustration for adults. The earliest castles in children's books, as well as those in books, films, and other works for children today, are thus part of a tradition that reaches back to the first printed books. If we look at manuscripts and other early images, the tradition extends even further back — to the building of real castles themselves.

Two distinct purposes — entertainment and instruction — shaped the development of children's books in the mid-eighteenth century. One influence on children's books was the popular and generously illustrated chapbook, intended primarily for the amusement of a wide and not very learned audience. In the crude woodcut prints that made the little books attractive to children as well as adults (even the illiterate), the castle appears most frequently as the residence of a giant or giants — and the place where their captives were imprisoned. One of the earliest chapbooks, *The pleasant and delightful history of Jack and the giants* (circa 1740), contains no fewer than four woodcuts of castle exteriors. In one woodcut many details of the castle can be picked out: turrets, portcullis, buttresses, and curtain wall, for example (fig. 72).

The second influence on the nascent children's book was the didactic publication. Books in this category had far more overt and weighty educational ambitions than the chapbooks; what entertainment they offered — much of it in the form of giants and castles — was sugarcoating on the pill of moral instruction.

Bunyan's *Pilgrim's Progress* (1678), for instance, was written for adults but always considered a suitable book for children. It reflects the traditional view of castles:

72
Woodcut illustration from
Jack and the Giants, *ca. 1800.*
Courtesy of the
Pierpont Morgan Library,
PML 81400

Christian is imprisoned by Giant Despair in Doubting Castle. Another giant's castle, from a children's book of 1780, *The British Champion; or Honour Rewarded,* is noteworthy not only for the detail and completeness of the castle-image but also for the fact that, although the castle plays a minor role in the text, it is the sole subject of the illustration (fig. 73).

Throughout the nineteenth century there were many more instructive books for children than there were works of fiction. But even in the realm of the didactic, castles made an early appearance when publishers realized the value of pictures in attracting attention. Some indication of the marketing power of the castle-image may be found in the title of a late eighteenth-century book: *The Prettiest Book for Children; being the history of the enchanted castle; Situated in the Fortunate Isles, and Governed by the Giant Instruction.* The eye-catching words enchanted, giant, and castle, coupled with an exotic setting, supported the further claim that the book was "written for the entertainment of Little Masters and Misses," but hardly disguised its soundly didactic foundation.

The single castle depicted in this book offers evidence of the by now archetypal nature of the castle-image (fig. 74). Although the text describes a French or Italianate palace, "a perfect square," with piazza, marble pillars, and formal gardens, the illustration shows a Norman-style defensive structure, with crenellated curtain wall, central keep, and corner towers. The illustration was, no doubt, enjoyed for its own sake, whatever pious message surrounded it, and it may have provided the only focus for imagination in a moralizing text.

In 1814, Thomas Love Peacock's popular *Sir Hornbook; or Childe Launcelot's Expedition, a Grammatico-Allegorical Ballad* appeared. The original edition boasted eight color plates, of which one was the castle of Sir Verb, besieged by Childe Launcelot and Sir Hornbook. (Peacock's witty point was that English syntax could be almost as impregnable as the English castle.) The castle-image here is associated not with giants, but with the legendary Middle Ages.

Castles also appeared in more strictly factual works for children in this period. The fine, clear image of a "Baron's Castle besieged by the Vassals of another Baron" in *Marshall's Abridgement of English History* (1801), however accurate and reportorial, must have provided an inspiration for many youthful fantasies. Pleasure and learning are also

or, Honour Rewarded. 47

till it began to grow dark, and then I tied my horse to a tree, and laid me down to sleep.

About break of day I awoke and mounted my horse. After a ride of near two hours, I thought I saw at a distance a large building; when I came nearer, I found it was a great and wonderful high castle. As I was

74 *Illustration from* The Prettiest Book for Children, *ca. 1795. Courtesy of the Pierpont Morgan Library, PML 81597*

The Enchanted Castle. 23

being (as he really is, though a giant) a very mild and tender-hearted person, he cannot endure, I suppose, that the blood of innocent animals should be shed for mere diversion; or else he thinks, perhaps, that if these creatures were to be suffered in the island they would spoil his gardens, of which he is indeed most remarkably fond. He would likewise be very angry if any person whatever should offer to disturb his birds, and much more if

B 4

73 *Illustration from* The British Champion, *ca. 1780. Courtesy of the Pierpont Morgan Library, PML 85661*

yoked together in *William's Tour with His Papa, or a peep into numbers, a nursery calculation, being the first rudiments of arithmetic* (1822). One of the illustrations in this combined tour book and mathematics text, is a view of Windsor castle, an appropriately solid English landmark for such a practical book.

Fantasy became increasingly common in children's books in the nineteenth century, and depictions of castles became more fanciful. A versified *Blue Beard* of 1850, for example, dresses its characters in Oriental costume, sets them amidst tropical vegetation, and adds a purely Gothic castle — with pointed arches, window tracery, and a delicate turret resting on a corbel. Gustave Doré's illustrations of Charles Perrault's fairy tales, with a half-dozen romantic and theatrical castles, appeared in 1862. The castle in *The Sleeping Beauty* (fig. 75), with its dramatic lighting and high, distant silhouettes of towers and pinnacles, symbolizes fantasy-land.

In American illustration, the castle took shape with a slightly different emphasis, between 1883 and 1910, in the pen-and-ink drawings of Howard Pyle. Pyle's renderings of sturdy castles for such books as *Otto of the Silver Hand* (1888) and *The Story of King Arthur and His Knights* (1902) and its three Arthurian sequels strengthened the legendary or quasi-historical aspect of the castle-image. Although Pyle did not know medieval castles or their ruins at first hand, his castles look as though they might in fact have existed. The drawing of Cameliard or Camelot (fig. 76) shows the convincing solidity of his work; it is easy to believe that King Arthur's castle looked this way.

Other illustrators of the same period tried for a similar "feel of stone" in their depictions of castles. H. J. Ford and his colleagues, Lancelot Speed, J. D. Batten, and G. P. Jacomb Hood, illustrated Andrew Lang's "color" fairy tale series (1889-1910). They were especially careful about architectural details — iron hinges, gratings, wards, wooden hoardings — since their focus, like that of many illustrators of fairy tales, was on characters at a near range, rather than on a more distant landscape.

Arthur Rackham also concentrated on characters, though his illustrations for the tales of the Brothers Grimm include several views of castles from a distance. The castle of the Sleeping Beauty (or *Briar Rose,* as the story is properly called), shows that Rackham allowed his fancy considerable rein (fig. 77). His castle rises magically out of its tangle of briars, set against a dramatic sweep of cloud.

75
*Illustration by
Gustav Doré, ca. 1862,
from* Les Contes
de Perrault.
*Courtesy of the
Pierpont Morgan
Library,*
PML 46605

Although the outer walls of Briar Rose's castle are sturdy, the structure above them has the earmarks of a fairy tale castle — delicate spired turrets and pinnacles, an open arcade, and pennons flying in the breeze.

The period just before and, for a short while, after the turn of the century is sometimes referred to as a golden age of fantasy illustration. Among those who contributed to the castle imagery of this period were Edmund Dulac, Kay Nielsen, Elsa Beskow, Helen Stratton, Louis Rhead, Harry Clarke, and Charles and W. Heath Robinson. Some produced restrained or quasi-historical images, while others showed Oriental palaces, in Moorish or Chinese style, as in *The Arabian Nights*. Still others drew or painted extravagantly romantic castles clinging to mountaintops, pushing clusters of slender spires into the clouds. Most of these castle types survive today in children's books. For example, John R. Neill's images in the later Oz books (fig. 78) show the kind of fantastic castle also popularized by Disney.

The changes in the castle-image coincided with the increased popularity of the fairy tale in the nineteenth century, and with the repeated publication of such tales by Perrault, the Brothers Grimm, Hans Christian Andersen, Peter Christen Asbjörnsen and Jörgen Möe, Andrew Lang, Joseph Jacobs, and others. In many cases, the tales were refined by the sophisticated hand of the editor or adapter. Fewer tailors and more princes, fewer giants' castles and more kings' castles, appeared. Even when the tale did not specifically focus on or mention a castle, the illustrator often assumed that the king, queen, or prince must naturally live in one, and so it appeared in the illustration. Castles appear in children's books outside the fairy tale context as well; in some cases they seem to have been used merely because they were thought to be appealing to children and appropriate for children's books.

What accounts for the interest in castles reflected in children's books and their illustrations? Perhaps the appearance of the castle itself explains its power over children and adults. Its grand scale, which dominates the landscape and alters one's sense of proportion, imprints the image on the viewer's mind. Built of stone, often situated on a rocky prominence, combining features of the natural and the man-made, the castle has an aesthetic attraction even for an unsophisticated taste. Like other large constructions, it is an achievement that seems to elevate all of human endeavor.

76
Pen and ink:
Two Knights Do
Battle Before Cameliard.
Howard Pyle, 1903.
Courtesy of the
Delaware Art Museum,
Howard Pyle Collection

Even young children are fascinated by the building arts; among their own earliest constructions are likely to be sand castles. Older children may appreciate the feats of engineering and architecture represented by the castle, and the scope it offered for ingenuity in planning, defense, and residential arrangements. Castles may be considered early and imposing examples of form following function, as the design of the building evolved to meet practical and military considerations.

Castles are often depicted as remote or isolated, belonging to a simpler and more natural world than that of modern, industrialized culture. In history and in children's fiction, castles belong to a period of active adventure when life was unpredictable, dangerous, and exciting.

To Americans, both children and adults, castles seem particularly romantic and exotic, both as symbols of the distant past and as reminders of the Europe left behind by

95

those who came to the New World. As the dwellings of aristocracy, castles carried some of the glamor of a stratified society to a nation that had resolved to sink all class-distinctions in democracy.

Perhaps the strongest appeal of castles is psychological. Although the castle may represent a mysterious, terrible authority, this is not the way castles are portrayed in children's books. Instead, the castle symbolizes security, safety, the home base from which one can make forays into the world with confidence. Like the wider symbolism of the fairy tale itself, the image of the castle feeds the child's longing for stability and permanence. The child becomes the prince or princess, his parents are the king and queen (or giant or ogre) of the tale, and every child's home is, quite literally, a castle whose impregnable walls enclose a world that can be dominated and controlled. Moreover, as the everyday world dwarfs the child, so the castle dwarfs the grown-up; in the oversized scale of the castle the relative advantage of adult height becomes less significant.

In fact, the castle is much less prominent in illustration than our childhood memories suggest. It is seldom the focus of illustration; instead, it is a "given" that can be reduced to a sketchy outline in the distance or suggested by a single element — door, tower, or parapet — in the foreground. Because illustrators are generally more interested in action than in landscape, there are many illustrations in which the castle is hinted at — by medieval clothing, furnishings, or armor — or merely implied by a massive wall or a distant silhouette.

Castles are structures to be filled or rebuilt by the imagination. The most fanciful castle-images, which defy gravity and the limits of engineering, reflect the child's sense of the infinite power of fantasy. So great is the appeal of this single symbol that the contemporary imagination, while it still looks back with longing to the castle of the historical past, has also looked to the future in search of the same constellation of symbolic qualities. The immense self-contained spaceship or space-station of *Star Wars* or *Star Trek*, a secure but remote outpost of power, is in a sense the castle transfigured.

77
Illustration: Briar Rose
by Arthur Rackham, 1909.
from Sixty Fairy Tales of
the Brothers Grimm

78
Illustration by J.R. Neill
from The Road to Oz,
by L. Frank Baum.
Courtesy of
Harvard College Library

The author would like to acknowledge the cooperation of the Pierpont Morgan Library, both in the work of research and in allowing some of the holdings of the Library to be reproduced here; she is especially grateful for the assistance of staff member Sharyl Smith in her search for material.

79
Pen and ink:
Robin Shooteth
His Last Shaft.
Howard Pyle, 1883.
From The Merry
Adventures of Robin
Hood.
Courtesy of the
New York Public Library,
Central Children's Room,
Donnell Library Center

Elizabeth H. Hawkes

Of
Knights and Castles:
Illustration by
Howard Pyle and
His Students

In late nineteenth- and early twentieth-century America, stories about the Middle Ages became enormously popular in books and magazines for both adults and children. The artists who illustrated these stories and novels shared a romantic view of the medieval past. Castles, knights, and other images that suggested the medieval appeared frequently in their work.

One of America's most popular storytellers during this period was Howard Pyle (1853-1911), a successful writer, teacher, and illustrator. Along with the work of Edwin Austin Abbey, Charles Dana Gibson, A.B. Frost, and many others, his pictures filled the pages of books and magazines. Pyle drew heavily upon the tradition of mid-nineteenth century English illustration ranging from the humorous drawings of John Leech and John Tenniel to the romantic pre-Raphaelite visions of Dante Gabriel Rossetti, John Millais, and Frederick Sandys. As a teacher, Pyle encouraged a generation of American illustrators including those with such distinct styles as N. C. Wyeth, Elizabeth Shippen Green, and Maxfield Parrish.

Though Pyle is often remembered as an interpreter of the American Colonial period, he also found serious inspiration for his writing and drawings in the Middle Ages. *The Merry Adventures of Robin Hood* (1883), one of Pyle's first books with a medieval subject, is a modern narrative based on the tradition of English folk tales and ballads. The main sources for Pyle's story of the popular outlaw-hero were two eighteenth-century publications: Joseph Ritson's anthology of old English ballads and Thomas Percy's collection of English and Scottish stories, which Pyle's mother had read to him during his childhood.[1]

Pyle's *Robin Hood* features twenty-three full-page drawings, and many of the chapters are decorated with headpieces and tailpieces (ornamental designs at the beginnings and ends of chapters). Often the illustrations have floral borders reminiscent of the work of designer and book illustrator Walter Crane, whose version of the Grimms' fairy tales was published in England in 1882. Crane was involved in the late nineteenth-century English

80

Ink on paper:
Away They Rode with Clashing Hoofs.
Howard Pyle, 1888.
Courtesy of the Delaware Art Museum,
Howard Pyle Collection

Arts and Crafts movement, led by William Morris, which attempted to preserve and perpetuate pre-industrial traditions in design and craftmanship.

The illustrations for *Robin Hood* are packed with details of the English countryside as Pyle imagined it: stone castles with round towers, half-timbered inns, and dense forests. This kind of detail is exemplified by the illustration "Robin Shooteth His Last Shaft" (fig. 79).

Pyle's *Robin Hood* was a landmark in American book design — a volume conceived as an aesthetic whole in which illustrations, text, typeface, and binding were unified in style and concept. Instead of being cut by hand on wooden blocks by an engraver, as was common at the time, Pyle's line drawings were reproduced photo-mechanically, thus taking full advantage of recent technological developments in printing. This new process eliminated the need for an intermediate step in which the engravers would re-draw, and possibly change, the artist's design. *Robin Hood* was a critical success on both sides of the Atlantic and even William Morris commended it, although he admitted his surprise that something of artistic value had come out of America.[2]

Robin Hood was followed by another tale inspired by medieval times, *Otto of the Silver Hand* (1888). The story tells of a gentle, motherless boy raised in a monastery and then returned to his father's castle in rivalry-torn Germany. Castle life is depicted in illustrations of children perched on the ledge of a high tower far above the castle's courtyard, and knights in full armor riding their horses across a stone bridgeway (fig. 80). Headpieces depict the castle where Otto was born and the monastery where he was raised. The story describes in detail Otto's castle with its massive stone walls and towers, the great gateway with a heavy iron portcullis suspended above its arched entrance, the central house where Otto's father lives, the tall narrow watch tower and wooden belfry, and the roadway winding up the rocky slope to the castle.

In 1892, Pyle's *Men of Iron* was published. The book recounts the adventures of a fifteenth-century English boy, Myles Falworth, who is forced to flee from his castle with his parents. By the end of the tale Myles, now a young prince, slays his father's enemy and returns to the castle not only vindicated, but also happily married. Pyle imaginatively portrays the exciting episodes of the story in the twenty-one black-and-white oils produced especially for the book.

81

Untitled illustration by Howard Pyle from Tennyson's The Lady of Shalott, *1881. Courtesy of the Delaware Art Museum Library*

At about the same time that these books appeared, Pyle was writing and illustrating numerous stories with medieval themes, most of which were published as serials in children's magazines. *Pepper and Salt* (1886) and *The Wonder Clock* (1888) were collections of fables, fairy tales, and poems that appeared first in *Harper's Young People.* Medieval settings are common in these works, and the illustrations show multi-towered castles, along with kings, princesses, magical animals, and even trolls. The cover of *Pepper and Salt* is embellished with a caricature of a medieval illuminated letter, and the frontispiece shows a jester (who looks remarkably like Howard Pyle as a young man) playing a pipe and reading to a group of children seated nearby. Stories from *The Wonder Clock* (one for each hour of the day) are told by Father Time and his grandmother; verses and drawings by Pyle's sister Katharine are included.

At the turn of the century, romantic adult fiction set in the medieval period came into vogue. Pyle had gained a national reputation as an illustrator of medieval subjects by the mid-1890s, and he was sought after by magazine editors. Among the stories illustrated by Pyle were Eugene Field's "The Werewolf," a tale of Yseult and Siegfried, for *Ladies' Home Journal* and Bret Harte's "Birds of Cirencester" for *Scribner's.* For *Harper's Monthly Magazine,* Pyle illustrated Mark Twain's "Saint Joan of Arc" and stories by James Branch Cabell, Justus Miles Forman, Brian Hooker, Marjorie Bowen, and others.

Though Pyle was usually gratified by public approval, he grew tired of repeating the same subjects and illustrating stories that he considered "the fake medieval type."[3] Pyle's standards were as high for the work of others as for his own. In fact, he wrote to the editor of *Harper's Monthly* to complain of having to make drawings for stories he felt had no permanent literary value. In his letter he argued that some of the stories were neither true to history nor very fanciful.[4]

In 1902, Pyle began to work on his own version of the legends of King Arthur. The project grew into a series of four volumes: *The Story of King Arthur and His Knights* (1903), *The Story of the Champions of the Round Table* (1905), *The Story of Sir Launcelot and his Companions* (1907), and *The Story of the Grail and the Passing of Arthur* (1910). The books were based largely on Sir Thomas Malory's fifteenth-century compilation of Arthurian tales (*Le Morte d'Arthur*).[5] Malory's tales were filled with murder,

82
Ink on paper: Headpiece for
"The Story of Sir Tristram
and the Lady Belle Isoult"
from The Story of the
Champions of the Round Table.
Howard Pyle, 1883.
Courtesy of the
Delaware Art Museum,
Howard Pyle Collection

betrayal, and wickedness, as well as noble chivalry, and Pyle tried to modify them for the children who were his main audience. His goal in the King Arthur books was to present the noble and worthy nature of his characters and to avoid the cruel, mean, and treacherous aspects.

The Arthurian legends were not new to Pyle. He was familiar with the stories from his childhood and, in 1881, as a young man, he had illustrated Tennyson's *Lady of Shalott* in which the heroine falls in love with Sir Launcelot and finally dies of unrequited love. Dressed in white and lying in a small boat, she floats downstream from her island to "many-tower'd Camelot," which Pyle depicts in full-color (fig. 81).

The King Arthur books are richly embellished with full-page illustrations, hand-lettered titles, illuminated initials, and decorative headpieces and tailpieces. Castles figure prominently in the drawings. The headpiece (fig. 82) for the tale of Sir Tristram in *The Story of the Champions of the Round Table*, for instance, shows Tristram's father, King Meliadus, with his hunting horn pursuing a magical stag to an enchanted castle on an island.

In the King Arthur series, in *Robin Hood*, and in his other works inspired by the Middle Ages, Pyle tried to create historically accurate settings, costumes, architecture, and other details. His drawings were based on his study of fifteenth- and sixteenth-century artists such as Albrecht Dürer, Hans Burgkmair, Lucas Cranach, and others. He also referred to such nineteenth-century works as James Planché's *Cyclopaedia of Costume* and Henry Shaw's volumes on the dress, furniture, decoration, architecture, and ornament of the Middle Ages. Pyle's personal library contained works on many aspects of medieval life and culture, all of which served as valuable source material for his illustration and writing.[6]

Certain objects and designs that appear in Pyle's illustrations can be traced directly to these sources. For example, the curved bracket on the enclosed wooden shelf, the crucifix, and the hour-glass in "Robin Shooteth his Last Shaft" (fig.79) appear to be based on Dürer's engraving, *St. Jerome in His Room*; the same is true of some objects that appear in *Otto of the Silver Hand* and *The Wonder Clock*.

Even though Pyle aimed for accuracy in detail, he did not pretend to recreate an exact time and place. In his Robin Hood and King Arthur books, his goal was clearly to entertain without sacrificing fidelity to his sources. King

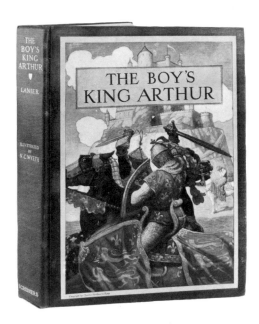

83
*Illustration by
N.C. Wyeth for*
The Boy's King Arthur,
*edited by Sidney
Lanier, 1917.
Courtesy of the
Delaware
Art Museum*

Arthur and many of Pyle's other characters were based on ancient legends, but Pyle humanized the characters, vividly described the countryside, and added details to make a more coherent story.

Pyle taught illustration at the Drexel Institute in Philadelphia from 1894 until 1900, when he opened an art school for a select group of promising students at his studio in Wilmington. Even when he became too busy to teach classes on a daily basis, he offered a weekly session of criticism for young illustrators. Pyle managed to pass on his abiding love of the Middle Ages to his students, many of whom also became notable illustrators of medieval themes. He encouraged them to immerse themselves deeply in their subjects in order to understand them fully. He also advised his students to compile picture-scrapbooks of costumes, architecture, furniture, and decoration that might be useful in preparing illustrations, and he recommended that the best sources for authentic details were original prints from the period under consideration.

Of all Howard Pyle's students, N. C. Wyeth (1882-1945) was probably the one most involved with medieval subjects. When he came to Wilmington to study with Pyle in 1902, he specialized in adventure stories with Western motifs. But as his career developed, his subjects became more varied. He illustrated a number of the Scribner Illustrated Classics series beginning with *Treasure Island* (1911). Several of the Illustrated Classics were stories of the medieval period, including Robert Louis Stevenson's *The Black Arrow* (1916), *The Boy's King Arthur*, edited by Sidney Lanier (1917), and *The Scottish Chiefs* by Jane Porter (1912). He also illustrated an edition of *Robin Hood* (1917).

Although Wyeth had not traveled to England and Scotland, which provided the settings for many of his medieval stories, he researched his subjects extensively by reading history and by examining photographs and drawings of the countries in which his scenes were set. In this way he followed Pyle's dictum that the detail of a story should be presented as accurately as possible.

One of Wyeth's most successful medieval subjects was *The Boy's King Arthur*, adapted by Sidney Lanier from Sir Thomas Malory's fifteenth-century compilation. Wyeth supplied fourteen full-page illustrations, a title page, a cover design depicting two knights fighting in front of a massive castle (fig. 83), and endpapers decorated with a procession of knights and maidens riding toward a castle.

84
Illustration:
It Hung Upon a Thorn
and There He Blew
Three Deadly Notes,
by N.C. Wyeth, from
The Boy's King Arthur.
Private Collection.
Photograph courtesy of
the Brandywine
River Museum

85
Pen and ink wash:
Humpty Dumpty.
Maxfield Parrish,
1896–97.
Courtesy of the
Syracuse University
Art Collections

Since Pyle's King Arthur series had already become a classic, Wyeth was faced with the problem of finding a different approach to the subject that his teacher had handled so imaginatively. Unlike Pyle's ink drawings, which were intended for black-and-white reproduction, Wyeth's illustrations were to be printed in full color, thereby allowing him to work in brightly colored oils.

Wyeth followed Pyle's approach by concentrating on the dramatic moment of a scene. In *It Hung Upon a Thorn, and There He Blew Three Deadly Notes* (fig. 84), for example, the Green Knight blows the long horn hung from the gnarled tree branch, calling three damsels to arm him with shield and spear for his fight with Sir Beaumains. Whereas Pyle had worked in a detailed style based upon his study of fifteenth- and sixteenth-century engravings of medieval subjects, Wyeth worked in a style reminiscent of the American Impressionism in vogue at that time, using bright colors and loose brushstrokes. The landscapes which form the backdrops of these dramatic scenes seem to be transplanted from the Chadds Ford, Pennsylvania, countryside where Wyeth lived and worked. In an interview with Joseph F. Dinneen in the *Boston Sunday Globe Magazine,* he explained how he projected himself into the past.

In my own life I try to live the life that I depict. Some may wonder how I can live the life of the 12th century, which most of my costumed romance represents. The costumes and accessories of the 12th century may be different, but the sunlight on a bronzed face, the winds that blow across the marshlands, the moon illuminating the old hamlets of medieval England, the rain-soaked travelers of King Arthur's day are strictly contemporaneous in feeling.[7]

Another artist whose fanciful works often centered on images of knights and castles was Maxfield Parrish (1870-1966), who attended Howard Pyle's classes at Drexel Institute briefly in 1894. Parrish illustrated a number of children's stories in a uniquely imaginative style, and shared Pyle's talent for presenting fanciful scenes and droll characters in a manner that fascinated children and adults alike.

Parrish achieved great popularity for his magazine covers, book illustrations, advertisements, posters, and murals which often included picturesque castles — if not as the dominant image, then as a detail in the background. Even his earliest works have a castle motif — for example, the mural *Old King Cole,* completed in 1895 for the Mask and

86
Opposite page.
Photogravure illustration:
Its Walls Were as of Jasper,
by Maxfield Parrish,
from Dream Days
by Kenneth Grahame, 1898.
Private Collection.
Photograph courtesy of the
Brandywine River Museum

87
Chromolithograph: The Dinky-Bird.
Maxfield Parrish, 1904.
Courtesy of the
Brandywine River Museum

88
Illustration:
He Gazed at Her, His Face Kindling,
by Elizabeth Shippen Green,
from "Tiphäine la Fée,"
by Warwick Deeping, 1906.
Courtesy of the Delaware Art Museum

Wig Club at the University of Pennsylvania, which shows the nursery-rhyme character seated on a throne in the interior of a castle through whose arched windows other castles can be seen.

Castles also appear in the background of his oil painting *The Sandman* (1896), which received an award of honorable mention at the Paris Exposition of 1900, as well as on the cover design of his first illustrated book, L. Frank Baum's *Mother Goose in Prose* (1897). For Baum's book, Parrish used a unique technique, combining ink drawing and collage. In one illustration (fig. 85) he cut the figure of Humpty Dumpty, the ledge, and the castle from a single piece of drawing paper, outlined them in ink, and glued them to a sheet of Rossboard, a commercially prepared paper board imprinted with patterns of dots and lines. Parrish then drew the trees and other details directly on the board. A consummate draftsman, Parrish also used photography as an aid in the preparation of illustrations by projecting images of his costumed models onto a sheet of paper or canvas, then tracing the image on that surface.[8]

Parrish's castles were fanciful and were not historically accurate renderings; instead, they represented imaginary, faraway places. The frontispiece for Kenneth Graham's *Dream Days* (1900) (fig. 86), shows a young child peeking into a magical land filled with the round towers and conical roofs of castles, knights riding in pairs on horseback, and an enchanting ship. The entire scene is whimsical, as is the accompanying story which tells of a child who visits a land of castles every day in his imagination. This book and its companion piece, *The Golden Age* (1899), which were intended for an audience of older children and adults, describe the dreams and escapades of the children of a comfortable English family.

One of Parrish's most popular illustrations, *The Dinkey Bird* from Eugene Field's *Poems of Childhood* (1904), shows a young child on a swing in front of a castle that represents "the land of Wonder-Wander, whither children love to go" (fig. 87). Another of Parrish's popular images was *Air Castles*, a cover for *Ladies' Home Journal*, in which a day-dreaming child blows large soap bubbles as imaginary castles float in the clouds. Both of these illustrations were issued as colored reproductions and were widely distributed, thereby enhancing Parrish's popularity.

Images of castles were also incorporated in the illustrations of some of Howard Pyle's other students. One of the most successful was Elizabeth Shippen Green who illustrated several romantic medieval stories for *Harper's Monthly Magazine*, with whom she had an exclusive contract from 1901 to 1924. *He Gazed at Her, His Face Kindling* (fig. 88) accompanied Warwick Deeping's love story ("Tiphäine La Fée") set in medieval Brittany. In Green's illustration the maiden Tiphäine pledges herself to Bertrand who has overthrown Tiphäine's unwanted suitor in a tournament. Bertha Corson Day, another of Pyle's students at Drexel, illustrated a book of fairy tales, *Where the Wind Blows* (1902), written by Pyle's younger sister, Katharine.

Green, Day, and some of Pyle's other students favored a decorative style in their work. Figures were reduced to flat, brightly colored shapes boldly outlined and placed against ornamental, patterned backgrounds. Networks of black lines filled in with colors suggest stained glass. This decorative style was drawn in part from the popular posters of the 1890s, from Walter Crane and the English Arts and Crafts tradition of illustration, and from Howard Pyle's own King Arthur drawings.

Howard Pyle nurtured the careers of many talented young artists. Like many great teachers, he did not force his students into a particular style but encouraged them to develop according to their own interests and strengths — and for such talented young students as Wyeth, Parrish, and Green, the era of the Middle Ages held a special appeal. Their interpretations, whether historically accurate or fanciful, were disseminated widely through book and magazine illustrations, as well as in commercial advertisements. Through their work medieval subject matter reached a broad audience and fired the imaginations of generations of book and magazine readers. In their illustrations the castle is a symbol of the past, of fantasy, and of a dream world — intimately associated with childhood, romance, fairy tales, and the make-believe.

Notes

KLINE / AGE OF CHIVALRY

1 Otto of Freising and Rahewin, *The Two Cities; A Chronicle of Universal History of the Year 1146 A.D.*, trans. C.C. Mierow, ed. A.P. Evans and P. Knapp (New York: Columbia University Press, 1928), p.45

2 Roberta D. Cornelius, "The Figurative Castle, A Study in the Medieval Allegory of the Edifice..." (Ph.D. diss., Bryn Mawr, 1930), pp. 16,64.

3 For discussion of the enchanted castle see Ruth Pfeiffer, "En route de vers l'au-delà Arthurien" (Ph.D. diss., Zurich, 1970).

4 Charles Coulson, "Structural Symbolism in Medieval Castle Architecture," *Journal of the British Archaeological Association* (1979): 79-90.

GROSS / CASTLE OF LOVE

1 James J. Wilhelm, *The Cruelest Month* (New Haven: Yale University Press, 1965), p.109.

2 *Le Siège du Château d'Amour*, Mémoires de la Societé des Antiquaires de France, t.I (1868), p. 184.

3 John Gower, *The English Works of John Gower*, ed. G.C. Macauley, 2 vols. (Oxford: 1900, 1901), EETS ES 81, 82, Book V, Lines 6573-74.

WELU / CASTLES ON MAPS

1 Similar symbols for towns are also found on some of the maps that accompany the Byzantine manuscripts of Ptolemy's *Geographia*. See, for example, the map of western Europe from a thirteenth-century Greek manuscript illustrated in L. Bagrow and R.A. Skelton, *History of Cartography* (Cambridge: Harvard University Press, 1964), pl. X.

2 See Fernao vaz Dourado's chart of the northern part of South America made in 1580, illustrated in color in *Die Karte als Kunstwerk: Dekorative Landkarten aus Mittelalter und Neuzeit* (Unterschneidheim: Verlag Dr. Alfons Uhl, 1979), no. 8.

3 Sir George Fordham, "Christopher Saxton, of Dunningley. His Life and Work," Thoresby Society's *Miscellany* 28 (1928), App. II, iv.

KLINE / GOTHIC REVIVAL

1 Charles Coulson, "Structural Symbolism in Medieval Castle Architecture," Journal of the British Archaeological Association *(1979): 81.*

2 Rose Macauley, *Pleasure of Ruins* (London: Thames and Hudson, 1966), p. 441.

3 A letter to Mary Berry, Friday, October 17, 1794. W.S. Lewis and A.D. Wallace, eds., *The Yale Edition of Horace Walpole's Correspondence*, XII (New Haven: Yale University Press, 1944.)

4 Edmund Burke, *A Philosophical Enquiry into the Origin of Our Ideas of the Sublime and the Beautiful*, edited with introductory notes by J.T. Boulton (New York: Columbia University Press, 1958).

5 Ann Radcliffe, *The Mysteries of Udolpho* (New York: Derby and Jackson, 1859), p. 179.

6 Ibid.

7 N. Wright, ed., *The Complete Works of Washington Irving: Journals and Notebooks* (Madison: University of Wisconsin Press, 1969), p. 55.

MILLER / GOTHIC NOVEL

1 Edmund Burke, *A Philosophical Enquiry into the Origin of Our Ideas of the Sublime and Beautiful*, ed. James T. Boulton (New York: Columbia University Press, 1958). The impact of Burke's essay was almost immediate — the phrase "the sublime and the beautiful" quickly entered everyday speech.

2 Mario Praz, "Introductory Essay," in *Three Gothic Novels: The Castle of Otranto, Vathek, Frankenstein*, ed. Peter Fairclough (Harmondsworth: Penguin Books, 1968), p. 10.

3 Quoted by Eino Railo, *The Haunted Castle* (New York, 1927; reprinted, New York: Gordon Press, 1974), p.5.

4 Warren Hunting Smith, *Architecture in English Fiction* (New Haven: Yale University Press, Yale Studies in English, 1934), p. 18.

5 The quotations are from Mrs. Parson's *Lucy* (1794), Mrs. Roche's *Trecothick Bower* (1814), and Maturin's *Fatal Revenge* (1807) and *The Milesian Chief* (1812).

6 Smith, *Architecture in English Fiction*, p. 1.

7 Railo, *The Haunted Castle*, p. 7.

8 Devendra P. Varma, *The Gothic Flame* (London: Arthur Baker, 1957), p. 218.

9 G. R. Thompson, "Introduction" in *The Gothic Imagination: Essays in Dark Romanticism* (Pullman, Wash.: Washington State University Press, 1974), p.4.

10 James M. Keech, "The Survival of the Gothic Response," *Studies in the Novel* (Summer 1974): 141

11 Quoted by Varma, *The Gothic Flame*, p. 15.

12 Joel Porte, "In the Hands of an Angry God: Religious Terror in Gothic Fiction," in *The Gothic*

Imagination, ed. G.R. Thompson, p. 48.

13 Barton Levi St. Armand, "The 'Mysteries' of Edgar Poe: The Quest for a Monomyth in Gothic Literature," in *The Gothic Imagination*, ed. G.R. Thompson, p. 68.

14 Leslie A. Fiedler, *Love and Death in the American Novel*, rev. ed. (New York: Stein and Day, 1966), pp. 131, 132.

15 Varma, *The Gothic Flame*, p. 3; St. Armand, "Quest for a Monomyth," p. 65.

WORKMAN / CASTLE DANGEROUS

1 Edgar Johnson, *Sir Walter Scott* (New York: Macmillan, 1970), I: 225.

2 Johnson, II: 1260

3 Allen Frazer, ed., *An Edinburgh Keepsake* (Edinburgh: University Press, 1971), p. 29; Trevelyan, *An Autobiography and Other Essays* (London: Longmans Green, 1949), p. 201.

4 R.J.C. Grierson, ed., *The Letters of Sir Walter Scott* (London: Constable, 1932-1937), VI: 266.

5 Walter Scott, *Castle Dangerous* (1831), Chapter VIII.

6 Richard Gill, *Happy Rural Seat* (New Haven: Yale University Press, 1972), p. 240.

7 Johnson, II: 841.

8 Johnson, II: 1262.

KRAUSE / ANTIQUARIAN TO ROMANTIC

1 The Reverend William Gilpin, *Observations Relative Chiefly to Picturesque Beauty made in the Year 1776 on Several Parts of Great Britain, Particularly the Highlands of Scotland* (London: R. Blamire, 1789), I: p. 25.

2 Quoted in Leslie Parris, *Landscape in Great Britain, c. 1750-1850* (London: Tate Gallery, 1973), p. 59.

3 Joseph Farington, *The Farington Diary*, ed. J. Grieg (New York: George H. Doran, 1923), pp. 242-243.

4 Cosmo Monkhouse, *Turner* (London: Sampson, Low, Marston, Searle and Rivington, 1879), p. 3.

5 John Ruskin, *Modern Painters*, vol. 3 (New York: DeFau, n.d.), p. 255.

6 Walter Thornbury, *The Life of J.M.W. Turner, R.A.* (London: Hurst and Blackett, 1862), I: 189.

7 Ruskin, *Modern Painters*, vol. 3, pp. 259-260.

PARRY / LANDSCAPE PAINTINGS

1 Under the rubric, "Proceedings of the American Lyceum," Cole's "Essay on American Scenery" was first published in the *American Monthly Magazine*, n.s. I, no. 1, January 1836, pp. 1-12. It has been reprinted twice in the twentieth century: first in John W. McCoubrey, ed., *American Art, 1700-1960; Sources and Documents* (Englewood Cliffs, N.J.: 1965), pp. 98-110, and more recently in Marshall Tymn, ed., *Thomas Cole: The Collected Essays and Prose Sketches*, The John Colet Archive of American Literature, 162 (1920), no. 7 (St. Paul: 1980), pp. 3-17.

2 Thomas Gray, *Elegy Written in a Country Church-Yard* (London, 1836), stanza IX.

O'GORMAN / BUILDING IN AMERICA

1 A.J. Downing, *A Treatise on the Theory and Practice of Landscape Gardening, Adapted to North America* (New York: Funk & Wagnalls, 1967).

HAWKES / KNIGHTS AND CASTLES

1 Charles D. Abbott, *Howard Pyle: A Chronicle* (New York: Harper and Brothers, 1925), pp. 8, 114. Thomas Percy's *Reliques of Ancient English Poetry* (London: J. Dodsky) was originally published in 1765, and Joseph Ritson's *Robin Hood: a Collection of all the Ancient Poems, Songs, and Ballads, Now Extant, Relative to that Celebrated English Outlaw* (London: T. Egerton and J. Johnson) in 1795. We do not know which editions Pyle actually consulted.

2 Joseph Pennell, *Graphic Arts* (Chicago: University of Chicago Press, 1921), p. 92.

3 Abbott, p. 124.

4 Abbott, p. 125.

5 Abbott, p. 128.

6 Pyle referred to the reproductions of old master prints in *Kulturgeschichtliches Bilderbuch aus Drei Jahrhunderten*, ed. Georg Hirth, 6 vols. (Leipzig: G. Hirth, 1881-90). Among the books in his library were: James Robinson Planché's *Cyclopaedia of Costume*, 2 vols. (London: Chatto and Windus, 1876-79) and seven works by Henry Shaw including his *Dresses and Decoration of the Middle Ages* (London: W. Pickering, 1843).

7 Douglas Allen and Douglas Allen, Jr., *N.C. Wyeth* (New York: Crown Publishers, Inc., 1972), p. 80.

8 Coy Ludwig, *Maxfield Parrish* (New York: Watson-Guptill Publications, 1973), pp. 25, 198. Ludwig discusses Parrish's technique and use of photography.

THE TEXT IN THIS BOOK WAS SET IN JANSON
WITH HEADINGS AND DISPLAY TYPE IN
CASLON 540 AND JANSON.
TYPESETTING BY
ARLENE GRECO AND EXPERTYPE, INC., NEW YORK.
PRINTING BY LECTURIS, B.V., EINDHOVEN.
BOUND IN THE NETHERLANDS.

BOOK DESIGN BY
PAOLA PIGLIA.